A SHORT BOOK ABOUT
KILLING

A SHORT BOOK ABOUT
KILLING

Rev. Dr. Sw. Shraddhananda
aka Sonya Jones

SACRED FEET

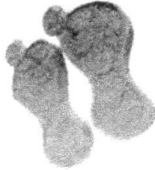

The Interfaith/Interspiritual/Intra-Tantric
Publishing Imprint of Slate Branch Ashram
The Jones Educational Foundation, Inc. (JEFI)
www.jonesfoundation.net

Published by SACRED FEET
The Interfaith/Interspiritual/Intra-Tantric
Publishing Imprint of Slate Branch Ashram
The Jones Educational Foundation, Inc. (JEFI)
A 501 (c) 3 Not-For-Profit Corporation
P.O. Box 289, Somerset, KY 42502, USA

PHOTO CREDIT
Rev. Dr. Sw. Shraddhananda: Melissa Reid

BOOK & COVER DESIGN
Sandra Simon Mangham

Printed in the United States of America
First published 2016

The SACRED FEET Publishing Imprint
Sw. Shraddhananda, Publisher
Sandra Simon Mangham, Managing Editor

ISBN: 978-0-9915010-5-2 (Paperback)
         978-0-9915010-6-9 (Kindle)

SACRED FEET Publishing Imprint Mission Statement

The SACRED FEET Publishing Imprint of Slate Branch Ashram is committed to the continuing development and refinement of the discipline of Interfaith Studies and Reflection. As such, SACRED FEET is devoted to bringing high quality Interfaith, Interspiritual, and Intra-Tantric manuscripts into print and appropriate digital formats. Manuscripts must analyze ideas or experiences from two or more religious and/or indigenous spiritual traditions in comparison or intersection with each other and must reflect intellectual as well as spiritual knowledge. SACRED FEET takes as its logo the Guru's *padukas*, or sacred sandals, a symbol indicating that subjects covered in submitted manuscripts must be handled with care and respect. However, manuscripts need not reflect the views of the publisher or editor. Electronic manuscripts with cover letters describing both the project under consideration as well as the author's spiritual journey and intellectual credentials are preferred.

Please contact: Swami Shraddhananda, Saraswati Order of Monastics, Publisher, or Sandra Simon Mangham, Managing Editor, at sacredfeetyoga@gmail.com.

A Tribute to Krzysztof Kieslowski (1941-1996)

Acknowledgements

I am deeply grateful for the work of Krzysztof Kieslowski—for his moral imagination and his art. Films like "The Decalogue," from which "A Short Film about Killing" was selected as a feature release, are much needed in an age when ethics have taken a backseat to entertainment.

I wish to thank Allegheny College for the sabbatical leave of absence 25 years ago which allowed me to spend time in the San Francisco Bay Area and attend the U.S. premier of "The Decalogue." To Sandra Simon Chamatkara Mangham, Managing Editor of The Sacred Feet Publishing Imprint, I daresay our years as professor and student at Allegheny inform the work we offer together now. Thank you for your intelligence, skill, and loyalty.

To the selections committee of the Parliament of the World's Religions 2015: Thank you for accepting my proposal and putting me in a position to follow through on what has been one of the most challenging projects of my long scholarly career. May the Parliament continue to grow and flourish. Likewise, may the Honors Program at the University of Kentucky which excused my presence during the writing of this book continue to attract the excellent students with whom I have had the pleasure to interact over the past eleven years.

Thanks to President Marcia Hawkins for her support and to Rev. David Miller for including *A Short Book about Killing* in "Conversations That Matter" and other programs on ethical issues at Union College.

Contents

Introduction

A Tribute to Krzysztof Kieslowski (1941-1996)

In May 1990, shortly after my first journey to India, I attended the U.S. premier of Krzysztof Kieslowski's "The Decalogue" at the San Francisco International Film Festival. Loosely based on the Ten Commandments, and made originally as a mini series for Polish television, "The Decalogue" has yet to be surpassed in my cinematic experience.

Composed of ten short films, the series has staying power for me because of the attention paid to ethical issues. "Decalogue V, A Short Film about Killing" (screenplay by Krzysztof Kieslowski and Krzysztof Piesiewicz), is particularly relevant now, 25 years after that initial viewing, when killing dominates the news.

Hence the title of this book, *A Short Book about Killing*, a tribute to both the ethical and artistic dimensions of Kieslowski's craft as well as a call to all who encounter it. Is it not time for us to examine the subject of killing with an eye toward greater understanding of this ominous topic?

"A Short Film about Killing" features a lone wolf who is seemingly motivated by self-hatred and the search for a thrill. This young male character wanders the streets of a Polish city until he finds a taxi driver to strangle. The killing takes some time as the 21-year-old drifter is far from being an accomplished murderer. In terms of motivation, his story recalls the narrative of Meursault, the protagonist in Albert Camus's short novel, *L'Etranger*, or *The Stranger*. When asked why he killed, Meursault says, in effect, "Je ne sais pas," or "I don't know."

Many killers in reality at large don't know their motives either, I suspect. They may need money for food or drugs. They may be blinded by ideology. They may be consumed by resentment and desire for revenge. Whether for personal gain or the reward of heaven, killers snuff out other lives that are not theirs to take.

The protagonist in Kieslowski's film, Jacek Lazar played by Miroslaw Baka, resembles the lone wolves who have manifested in young men such as Cho at Virginia Tech and Chris Harper-Mercer in Roseburg, Oregon. He is not a despicable character, but he is clearly lost and self-absorbed. Thus, he is vulnerable to stepping over the line into a dark world in which tasting the thrill of blood is more compelling to him than continuing to live in misery while honoring the laws of society.

Set in Warsaw, "A Short Film about Killing" also addresses the problem of the death penalty. The killer has no money. He is assigned to a defense attorney, Piotr Balicki played by Krzysztof Globisz, who is outraged by his client's being sentenced to execution by hanging. To no avail, the idealistic lawyer, recently out of law school, tries until the last moment to persuade the judge to overturn Jacek's sentence. It is difficult to discern if Piotr's anger originates in his opposition to capital punishment, worries about losing his first case, or both. Such is Kieslowski's genius. His characters are profoundly three-dimensional, their actions far too complex to be attributed to a single motive.

When the moment for the hanging arrives, Jacek's executioners offer him a cigarette. A filtered smoke won't do. He wants, and asks for, an unfiltered drag or two. His sense of entitlement is reminiscent of Meursault, unmoved by his mother's death, smoking and drinking coffee by her coffin. It also recalls scenes prior to the killing when Jacek's behavior is wantonly destructive. He pushes a rock off a bridge onto a freeway below and causes two cars to collide. He splatters food on a cafe window. Nearing his execution, Jacek confesses to an incident from his past in which he inadvertently caused his sister's death while drunk. This incident may be responsible for the murder he committed; it may have contributed to his selfishness.

Those responsible for Jacek's execution by hanging have a means of killing at their disposal far less sophisticated than the excruciating lethal injections now used in the United States. In a scene as powerful as the killings for which he must pay, Jacek is dragged whimpering to his death. Unsurprisingly, "A Short Film about Killing" was instrumental in overturning the death penalty in Poland.

Nothing about "A Short Film about Killing" is sensationalized. Shot in black and white, it is a supremely good example of an art film directed by a filmmaker on par with the great Swedish director Ingmar Bergman. In his foreword to the published screenplays which constitute "The Decalogue," Stanley Kubrick called the ability of Kieslowski and Piesiewicz to dramatize their ideas "dazzling."

Influenced by Kieslowski's early work as a documentarian, the film's intent is not to shock, but to bring the topic of killing as a serious ethical infraction into stark relief. In fact, Kieslowski belonged to a group of filmmakers who were concerned about moral anxiety. In an age in which morals are frequently seen as boring intrusions into a Roman-like arena in which the senses enjoy exaggerated play, Kieslowski's treatment of the commandment against killing asks us to examine the topic over and beyond our sense of adventure as timeless gladiators drawing our weapons.

Simply said, "A Short Film about Killing" is prophetic of the murders we have witnessed since Columbine. In its utter simplicity, it makes the high budget killer-thrillers produced in Hollywood look like what they are: movies designed to manipulate people into buying tickets to high definition portrayals of the iconic gun.

During that initial viewing of "The Decalogue," from which "A Short Film about Killing" was released as a feature film, I encountered an eminent San Francisco psychiatrist who watched the showings with me over strong coffee at the Kabuki Theatre (later purchased by Robert Redford's Sundance Cinemas). I persuaded Dr. Francis Rigney to write an analysis of "The Decalogue" for a special issue of *Film Criticism* which Prof. Lloyd Michaels, founder of the journal and a colleague at Allegheny College, had invited me to edit on psychoanalysis and cinema. One of my doctoral tracks at Emory was in the history of psychoanalysis as a "grave philosophy," Sigmund Freud's description of his system. I taught interdisciplinary seminars in psychoanalysis and literature at Allegheny, and drawing on my experience prior to doctoral studies, trained journalists. To my knowledge, Dr. Rigney's essay was the first feature length analysis of "The Decalogue" published anywhere in the world.

"The moral message of Kieslowski's film is clear," Dr. Rigney wrote, refusing to reduce the filmmaker's intentions to psychoanalytic jargon. "Nothing justifies killing fellow human beings."

Kieslowski was very much on my mind when I proposed a session entitled "A Short Seminar about Killing" to the Parliament of the World's Religions for meetings to be held in Salt Lake City in October 2015. As the

Parliament selections committee received thousands of proposals, I was gratified when "A Short Seminar" was one of the first to be accepted, especially given the prominence of killing on a global scale.

At the presentation itself, the audience appeared to be grateful for a safe space in which to explore the subject of killing. Some were shy at first. Some were angry about so many killings. More than one was concerned about the media's role in the drama of killing as well as manipulation of the airwaves by technologically adept Jihadists.

In *A Short Book about Killing,* we will necessarily raise questions about the possible impact the press plays in fueling the constant flow of murders. Although we should be grateful to reporters for keeping us informed, producers might be well advised to examine the format in which killings are delivered, especially on cable news. It may not be necessary to carry a killing on for several days, and then again, continuing coverage of one killing may actually prevent another from happening.

Killing, of course, is not new. Contrary to popular opinion, ISIS did not invent it. Killing stretches back to the beginnings of recorded history and saturates the literature made by the greatest minds of our race. Understandably, virtually all the world's religions inveigh against killing. The early Hindu and Jain teachers as well as Moses and the Buddha must have seen something fearful in the human psyche. Freud confirmed their suspicions with his theory on *thanatos,* the death instinct.

Of notable exception to the global religious stance against killing is radical Islam. Jihad is an anomaly among the world's religions. Although moderate Muslims, many of whom have been westernized, interpret jihad to mean "the battle within," radical Islam traces instructions to kill the

Heathen back to its founder, the last of the great Prophets, and to the *Quran*, which Muhammad is said to have received by transmission.

Although the human race would surely benefit by imbibing the first Buddhist precept, "No Killing," an epilogue to the drama of killing appears not to be anywhere in sight. By keeping Krzysztof Kieslowski's sensitive portrayal of both victim and killer alive, it is my distinct hope we can grow in our understanding and respect for human life.

May this tribute to the great Polish filmmaker Krzysztof Kieslowski help to diminish the killings which have claimed attention worldwide, particularly since September 11, 2001, and caused so much pain for the families of those whose lives have been terminated abruptly. May those who have lost their lives to the randomness and "ideology of bullets," so-called by a French official following the Paris attacks in Nov. 2015, rest in peace.

CHAPTER I

OVERCOMING THE DENIAL OF KILLING

My interest in the subject of killing, if *interest* is the right word, gained momentum in Feb. 2015 before the Paris attacks in November, before the San Bernardino Massacre shortly thereafter, when a respected professor of social work at Union College in Kentucky, where I serve on the Board of Trustees, was murdered by her 16-year-old son.

Supposedly a nice young man who was no problem to anyone, Jason Hendrix apparently snapped when his mother took away his computer and cell phone privileges. Jason also killed his father Kevin and younger sister Grace, age 12, before fleeing to Baltimore, Maryland, where he was killed himself in a fire fight with police.

A graduate of Union College, class of 1969, I felt unspeakable sorrow when I heard about Prof. Sarah Hendrix's death. Both my mother and father were graduates of Union as well—we form a triple legacy—and I have thought repeatedly how glad I am my parents did not live to see mass murders become almost routine in American society.

My father was never the same after fighting in World War II, my grandmother said. Something happened to him in Germany. Dad fought in the Battle of the Bulge, one of the bloodiest in the European theater, and he didn't want to talk about it much. When he did, he simply said he was lucky to have made it home alive.

Union had a memorial service, and Lizzie, a Hendrix daughter who was away at Berry College in Rome, Georgia, north of Atlanta, came to Kentucky for the funeral. Lizzie's brother Fred lives in Lexington where services were held for Sarah, Kevin, Grace, and Jason at Northeast Christian

Church. Lizzie lived with her family in Lexington before they moved to Corbin where her mother, father, and sister were killed. Somehow, according to the Dean of Student's Office at Berry College, Lizzie managed to graduate after the shootings.

Prof. Hendrix's death was not one of those high profile murders which the national networks turn into a media event. It was not a Columbine or Aurora, Colorado, Sandy Hook, Connecticut, Charleston, South Carolina, or Roseburg, Oregon. In terms of celebrity, the Sarah Hendrix killing was covered by both CNN and *USA Today,* but it did not turn into the spectacle which often characterizes mass murders. Sarah Hendrix was laid to rest as one of 88 to 92 people who are killed daily by guns in the United States of America.

Not to be redundant, but Prof. Sarah Hendrix was *one of 88 to 92 people who are killed daily by guns* (italics, mine) in the United States of American, these numbers compliments of CNN. As startling as this number may be, the word *daily* nearly jumps off the page when added to it. Yearly, the killings add up to about 30,000, Rep. Gabrielle Giffords' husband, former astronaut and space shuttle commander Mark Kelly, told CNN during a Dec. 4, 2015 newscast. "The United States has a serious problem with gun violence," Kelly added. He should know since his wife, Rep. Giffords (D-AZ) was shot in the head on Jan. 8, 2011 at a supermarket near Tucson where six other were killed, 13 wounded. Fortunately, she survived.

According to an article entitled "Behind the Bloodshed," written by Paul Overberg et al. for *USA Today,* family killings in the United States account for 52 percent of the total. Further, Overberg said, mass killings happen about every two weeks, but police do not always report them. Two-thirds of the 30,000 killed yearly are suicides, reliable sources claim, and one-third are homicides. Whereas the overwhelming number of suicides are White, most of the homicides are African-American and Hispanic.

During the summer months following the Sarah Hendrix murder, some time passed before I felt ready to begin the project on killing I had proposed to the Parliament. Since my proposal was accepted early, ample time allowed anxiety to ferment and delay the start of my research and writing. As many times as I considered beginning, I did not formally do so until late August. Parliament sessions were scheduled for October.

I found the subject of killing to be off-the-charts daunting. Every time I opened my computer to type, I looked for distractions. Denial kicked in when I tried to type, and I fled to the fitness center, my pontoon boat, or the grocery store—any place I could find to avoid the subject. Subliminally, I felt a grinding tension. As one who meditates, I normally enjoy a continuous sense of contentment, but thinking about killing clearly was jeopardizing my peaceful state of mind. I wanted to run away from the presentation I had proposed to the Parliament. I considered canceling.

My denial was much the same, I would imagine, as the denial experienced by other human beings who have difficulty believing they live in a country where 88 to 92 people are killed daily by guns—where a young White man can talk his way into a Bible study group at an historic African American church in Charleston aiming to blow everyone in the room to bits.

Finally, one morning after the murder of an aspiring young TV journalist and her camera man in Virginia, I woke up from my numbness and began to write. The killings at

WDBJ, Roanoke, were the tipping point for me as I had spent nearly 20 years training journalists at Allegheny College. That the lives of two such promising talents as Alison Parker and Adam Ward were terminated on a TV set by shooter Vester Flanagan, himself a frustrated TV reporter who could not seem to make the grade, was very difficult for me to absorb—even though I used to wonder in the 1960s when the next assassination would happen on TV for all the world to see. I shall never forget the day when news of President John F. Kennedy's having been shot in Dallas came over the loudspeaker at my high school in south central Kentucky, about an hour from Union College.

Actually, the first killing I came close to witnessing happened in reality, not on TV, when I was much younger, nine years old to be exact. As one of several baby boomers who grew up on a tree-shaded street in Somerset, where the population sign read 7,999 in 1957, I was playing outside down the street from my house one Spring evening when I heard a loud noise. At first, I thought the racket came from a hot rod muffler. I was ambling barefoot in the rain water running in the gutter across from Police Chief Harold Catron's house when a black Buick carrying his assassins sped away. To my knowledge, Chief Catron's killers were never found although one suspect committed suicide some time after.

Forty-five years later, Police Chief Catron's son Sam was murdered as well. Sheriff of Pulaski Co., Sam was well-respected as was his father. Sheriff Catron was the victim of a political intrigue. How his killers could have imagined, even for a minute, they could get away with shooting Sam Catron is still a mystery to me. At the time, following early retirement from Allegheny, I dipped back into journalism for awhile and wrote some features for the local newspaper, the Somerset *Commonwealth-Journal*. I wrote a remembrance of Sam, and I can still see him as a small boy, the youngest child in his family, running through the yard where his father was shot on the front porch of the Catron home.

When Sam was shot at a fish fry out at Shopville, where my mother used to teach and I, at age four, served as mascot of the varsity cheerleaders, I was in attendance at a Board meeting of the Master Musicians Festival, a cultural event for which Somerset is well-known across the Southeast. Someone on the Board must have received a phone call, because we turned on the radio to try and get some news. We didn't meet much longer that night. The sadness was palpable.

Police Chief Harold Lewis Catron was also shot in April, 45 years earlier. As the poet T.S. Eliot wrote, "April is the cruellest month." When murders like these two happen to good people, it is easy to think we are, indeed, living in the "waste land" Eliot imagined in his celebrated poem by the same name.

Are we a nation of killers? I began to wonder after the Sarah Hendrix murder. Are we as uncivilized as we appear to be? If we trace our history back to the arrival of the pilgrims on northeastern shores and the migration westward across Native American territory, we almost have to ask this question, don't we? It took a long time for historians to come to grips with the genocide of indigenous people in the United States. Where killing is concerned, denial cuts a large swath.

Dave Grossman must have been pondering a similar question when he researched and wrote *The Psychological Cost of Learning to Kill,* but Grossman, a military historian who never actually fought in a war, made a startling discovery through interviews and the like: Soldiers on the battlefield sometimes have to be prodded into pulling their triggers.

Did my father decline to shoot a Nazi? Or, did he suffer from having shot too many of Hitler's men? Sometimes, Dad would sit for hours, smoking little Camels, saying nothing. Mother wanted to see the land where her husband, brother, and father had fought, so she and I went on a tour to Germany and Austria sponsored by our church. Dad declined to go with us. "No way," he said. He was a nervous wreck the whole time we were gone.

Grossman seems to think we are not "Natural Born Killers," the title of a 1994 movie by Oliver Stone (screenplay by Quentin Tarantino) featuring the rampage of a serial killing couple, both traumatized in early life, who appear not to have a conscience. Granted, there is a big difference between men huddled in foxholes trying to defend their country and killing as pictured on the silver screen, supposedly as black comedy. I don't know if Woody Harrelson ever fought in a war, but I suspect if he had, he might have thought twice about taking the role of Mickey Knox in "Natural Born Killers." All dressed in white, Harrelson was made to look like an angel for the cover of *Breathe* magazine. He is almost as sweet-faced as Juliette Lewis in her role as his killer wife Mallory *Knox*, also the name of a Kentucky county where Union College lost an esteemed professor.

The big question with Jason Hendrix is: why? Peggy Munke, a close friend of Sarah Hendrix as well as director of the social work program at Murray State University, told the Louisville *Courier-Journal* she thought Jason, one of two adopted Hendrix children, probably acted out of shame rather than anger. He was thought to be a "perfect" young man by many in his Corbin, Kentucky community, and when his mother took away his computer and cell phone privileges, he probably could not deal with being called out. Were Jason Hendrix, in fact, motivated by shame, his behavior would speak to the existence of conscience, and the killing of his parents, the authority figures in his life, would read as anything but random. Jealousy of his younger sister, the first family member Jason killed, is also being investigated as a possible motive, according to an article by Dean Manning in *The Mountain Advocate*.

Conscience is an important consideration in any question about killing as well as in religion's role in prompting or stopping the bullets from flying. As is complicity. I didn't want to work on the very project I had proposed to the Parliament, because each time I began to work, I felt complicit with the band of consciousness which keeps the killings in motion.

Are we, in fact, complicit with the killings when we watch TV or read about them in the papers? Or, purchase what has come to be called "murderabilia?" Artifacts belonging to killers such as Charles Manson or the Son of Sam may make interesting "conversation pieces," but they also tend to evoke uneasy feelings in people who have negative associations with them.

When I was a child, I played with a holster and Army jackets my father and grandfather brought back from Germany. Years later, as a first year graduate student of literature and linguistics at the University of Louisville, I didn't think much about hanging a Nazi flag in my studio apartment as a room divider. My friends did not react to the red and black, fringed cloth one way or another, but when Dad came to visit, he immediately wanted to know why this emblem of atrocity was hanging in his daughter's quarters. In retrospect, I think seeing the Nazi flag on home turf hurt Dad's feelings, but at the time, I was a budding intellectual, and in my view, a "cultural artifact" was nothing more than that.

Going on five decades later, my attitude has changed. I would no more hang a Nazi flag in my private residence or ashram than I would display a flag associated with the Khmer Rouge or ISIS. I am glad my parents sold the Nazi sword I played with as a child, so I am not faced with disposing of it. "We live in a forest of symbols," wrote the French poet Charles Baudelaire, and symbols have power. As a symbol, rather than a mere "cultural artifact," a Nazi flag represents the killing of millions.

In the 1990s, I had the good fortune to join my Guru, my spiritual teacher, on tour in Poland. Her teachings were held in Lodz where Krzysztof Kieslowski is buried. I also spent some time in Warsaw, and it was great to gain a sense of the geography in which Kieslowski filmed his masterpiece, and where his famed apartment building is located. While in Warsaw, I encountered a young man who identified himself as a neo Nazi. I did not launch into a diatribe incorporating the Sixth Commandment, "Thou Shalt Not Kill," against him, but neither did I offer to buy his items for sale.

Definitely, there are degrees of complicity. I still have the holster I played with as a child, the one Dad wore in Germany, but I do not romanticize it, or have it on display. I was planning to offer his gun rack to Union College to use as a kind of "trophy case" in honor of the scholarship my family foundation endowed in his honor. After the Sarah Hendrix murder, however, I am re-thinking this gift. A gun rack is a gun rack, after all, and even if it houses certificates of achievements, it still has symbolic power.

Likewise, how we receive the news matters in the universal scheme of things. Watching the evening news, for instance, does not have the same energetic force as staying glued to the television with reportage of the latest killing in process. If we focus unduly on the negativity inherent in such coverage, we become complicit with the killings, whether we intend to or not. At the same time, if we try to ignore them, or deny them, we are complicit, too, as pushing their explosiveness into unconscious depths allows them mindless power over us.

In news coverage of virtually all killings, talk turns inevitably to criminology, politics, and mental health. What motivated the killer? reporters ask much as I inquired in the case of Jason Hendrix. Should anyone who wants to own guns be allowed to buy them? Is the mental health system in the United States so poor that disturbed individuals can purchase guns as easily as crystal meth or heroin? Rarely, if ever, does anyone mention the 6th Commandment: "Thou Shalt Not Kill."

In coverage of all the killings I have watched on TV, the 6th Commandment—"Thou Shalt not Kill"—has never been mentioned once. Perhaps we are in denial about the existence of religious injunctions against killing. Or, ignorant. Then again, perhaps television producers and reporters fear being identified with the Religious Right, and they take extra good care to adhere to the separation of church and state.

After he shot three family members, Jason Hendrix attended a Bible study group at Forward Community Church, a non-denominational congregation he had joined with his parents. No one detected anything different about Jason's behavior. He mentioned the guitar he was learning to play, and a book entitled *God's Not Dead*. He said nothing about the six guns he had loaded and packed in his mother's SUV.

It is, perhaps, time for news reporters to ask some questions derived from the world's religions. That killing violates the 6th Commandment as well as the Hindu/Jain law of *ahimsa*, "hurt no living thing," and the Buddhist precept, "No Killing," certainly comes through in the grief expressed by mourners of those whose deaths are covered by the national media. There's no denying their pain.

In terms of religion, it may be time, as well, for news reporters to learn more about radical Islam rather than accepting what the so-called experts say at face value. Significant differences exist between the Jihadists and moderate Muslims who live and worship at the far end of the continuum from the mass killings we have experienced worldwide.

Then again, are moderate Muslims immune to the romance of the caliphate on the Internet? The stories of young women who have managed to slip away from their homes to join up with ISIS would suggest not. According to a Nov. 17, 2015 article by Danielle Paquette in *The Washington Post,* an estimated 4,500 Westerners have departed for the Islamic state. The average age is 21. One in seven is female.

Shortly before Sarah Hendrix was murdered by her son in Corbin, Kentucky, a man threw his five-year-old daughter off a bridge in St. Petersburg, Florida, and in the same time period, another mass shooting of eight or nine— numbers varied—occurred out West. These killings happened ten months before a Jihadist couple wiped out 14 people in San Bernardino, California with an A-15 assault rifle, also known as "America's Gun."

.

CHAPTER II

A KILLING AT THE DAKOTA

In the Summer of 1981, I felt a shiver akin to a premonition. In New York City for a huge political rally, I was standing outside the Dakota when a friend said, "This is where John Lennon was killed." The shiver made sense.

Lennon was shot four times in the back by Mark David Chapman who eventually pleaded guilty. God told him to kill Lennon, he said. Still in prison as of Dec. 8, 2015, the 35th anniversary of Lennon's death, Chapman has been denied parole eight times.

This may sound sadistic, but certain Lennon fans feel that Chapman should be kept in jail past his last heart beat. He murdered the man who taught a generation to imagine a world without killing.

Like many young women my age in the 1960s, I went wild over the Beatles. I got to see the now classic Ed Sullivan Show on which the Beatles appeared, hot from England, when it aired live on Feb. 9, 1964. For a time, "I Wanna Hold Your Hand" was my anthem. I played it over and over again on the Briar Bowl jukebox for a nickel a spin. In retrospect, I would bet the repetition of lyrics made the women in my bowling league more than a little nervous. At sweet sixteen, however, as a queen of bell bottomed jeans, I could not see why anyone would not want to swoon over Lennon and the boys from Liverpool.

As the Beatles progressed from teeny bopper rock to complicated musical strains, some Indian, so did my friends and I. In college, we were definitely still listening, but in the years of Sgt. Pepper, we traded in our innocence for existential disassociation. The times demanded that we step out of our lonely hearts and into the streets to march for equality and freedom.

Perhaps we should grant him the right to swoon, too, but the thought of Mark David Chapman getting naked and obsessing over "The White Album" could cause more than a shiver up the collective spine. At one point, Chapman performed his nude ritual and prayed to Satan for the courage to murder John Lennon.

He became a religious fanatic, and when he found out that Lennon said the Beatles were more famous than Jesus, he felt betrayed. Increasingly, he came to see Lennon as a phony, a traitor to Holden Caulfield's brand of alienation. Eventually, Chapman obliterated Caulfield, too, by ripping up his copy of *The Catcher in the Rye*.

Many of us were hooked on J.D. Salinger. I rolled around the Southeast in a 1965 bronze Mustang I christened Seymour. If that Mustang, wherever she is now, could give voice, she would croon a tune of eight-track tapes dubbed from the Temptations and the Supremes. For some reason, I never listened to the Beatles while driving. Motown was more to my liking on the road with Jack Kerouac. But, I would give the 1964 and a half red Mustang convertible with a 230 engine I have in storage, a gift from my dad, to wind the tape backwards and slap that gun out of Chapman's hand.

By his own admission, Mark David Chapman wanted to be John Lennon. Chapman was a pudgy kid from Atlanta, very different looking from the skinny killer Jacek in "A Short Film about Killing," and from John Lennon. Chapman admired celebrities and wanted to be one himself. He considered killing other stars, too, but ultimately, it was Lennon who bore the brunt of five bullets fired from a .38 caliber pistol. One shot failed to hit its mark. The errant bullet is lodged in memory as a tribute to the life Lennon could have lived with Yoko and Sean, five years old when his father was gunned down.

Mark David Chapman, that's the problem with killing. It robs another human being of his breath, his love, his song.

In those days, assault rifles hadn't yet appeared on the scene as weapons of mass destruction. Even Lee Harvey Oswald used a mail order rifle with a scope to hit President John Kennedy riding in a convertible in downtown Dallas. Oswald's weapon was primitive compared with the A-15s used 35 years after Lennon's death to remove 14 people in San Bernardino, California from the planet. But, they weren't celebrities—except in the hearts of their loved ones.

Shooting John Lennon expelled the evil inside him, Chapman said. Could this be the same kind of release a Jihadist feels when he mows down an Infidel? Lennon was an imperialist in Chapman's mind. No question, Chapman gave him the power to colonize his thoughts. When we surrender our sense of right and wrong to a rock star or an ideology, we put ourselves in a position to be guided by the committee Chapman described whether we identify the voices we hear as Satan or sex or Allah.

As I watched the CNN special entitled "Killing John Lennon," I was grateful to learn that Lennon had an awakening before his death. George Harrison had taken a turn east, and his solo work reflects his peace. The other Beatles carried on through ups and downs and divorces. That Lennon struggled with alcohol and drugs is no secret. "I hope to go first," he told an interviewer, "I don't know what I would do without Yoko."

Caught in a squall while sailing to Bermuda, Lennon suddenly came to grips with his own malaise. He hit bottom, and the awakening shows in his face. In photographs taken after he took up an acoustic guitar and began to sing again, his smile is radiant. His boat had landed safely at last.

For as long as you live, Mark David Chapman, and into the great beyond, you will never take the music away from John Lennon.

CHAPTER III

FEELING SORRY FOR THE KILLERS

For many people, it is difficult to feel compassion for killers. The most immediate tendency is to try and repress their deeds, and then, denounce them. Words such as "horrific" and "heinous" help us to keep from looking at the killings squarely and seeing them clearly. The frequency with which these words are used in news reports tends to create a veil of numbness. Name-calling also can feed into the process of demonization, and it can help us to block our own sadness. Rarely, if ever, have I heard anyone say, "I feel sorry for the killer, too."

Admittedly, I continue to struggle with Mark David Chapman, John Lennon's killer, and with what appears to be his arrogance. "The very sight of him makes me want to puke," I heard someone say. That anyone could be so "audacious" as to seek fame for such a "hideous" act is "appalling." Words like these help to assuage our discomfort. Far better to be an anonymous cog in the great wheel of existence than to be remembered for shooting any soul in the back, much less a man who gave so much to humanity.

Musicians and children have a way of touching down deep to the levels beneath our judgments and justifications. Thus, John Lennon's death still troubles me as do the murders of JonBenet Ramsey, Adam Walsh, Baby Bella, and 20 children in a town just north of New York City with 20 more down south in Atlanta.

"Every time I think about those kids" in Newtown, "it gets me mad," said President Barack Obama on "Guns in America," a CNN special hosted by Anderson Cooper Jan. 7, 2016.

On a wintry day in Dec. 2012, a 21-year-old shooter named Adam Lanza killed a total of 28 people in Newtown, Connecticut. In addition to 20 first graders at Sandy Hook Elementary School, Lanza shot seven adults, including his mother, before killing himself.

Do I feel sorry for Adam Lanza? Not a chance. But, I do feel compassion. I cannot afford to feel otherwise and stay in contact with the capacity for forgiveness which prevents me from becoming a killer myself. Imagine a monk with a grudge against a young man who hated himself so much that he blasted his way out of life, taking 28 others with him. It is rarely easy, but the monastic challenge is to love everyone equally, killers included.

Any killing, seen from a religious perspective, constitutes a sacrifice, wrote Rene Girard in his now classic text, *Violence and the Sacred*. How might Girard's assertion apply to the mass murders of late? Were the children at Sandy Hook sacrificed like young lambs to a God who is angry with a culture that has turned its back on him? Were the teenagers at Columbine symbolic sacrifices, or representatives of young people living in an age when suicide seems to be more popular than the senior prom? Were the people attending a concert and enjoying open air cafes in Paris, along with the writers at *Charlie Hebdo* nine months previously, Heathen sacrifices to Allah? Did Adam kill Nancy Lanza as a sacrifice, or as a tribute to his mother's enthusiasm for guns?

Killing a parent was once the definition of tragedy writ large. Tragedy may be impossible in an age when people are reduced to automatons, literary critics and sociologists insisted throughout the 20th century. From the time of the Greek classics, familial conflict has driven our literary texts. Sigmund Freud dealt extensively with the so-called Oedipal and Electra dramas in which offspring seek to kill off a parent in the quest for psycho-sexual maturity. But, Freud died in 1939 well before the psychic situation was complicated by children committing suicide after killing their parents.

Freud also posited the existence of a super-ego in each human being. The super-ego, said the father of psychoanalysis, is made up of what we are taught about right and wrong by our families, religious institutions, and cultures. In the case of Adam Lanza, we probably could say the super-ego broke down, or lost its grip on his psyche. When the super-ego is functioning, it can act as a barrier to killing, but where Jason Hendrix is concerned, an overly wrought super-ego could have provoked the murder of both parents.

In addition to children killing their parents, mothers sometimes confess to killing their children. An estimated 200 women kill their children yearly in the United States, but not all are caught or confess. A study conducted by Dr. Phillip Resnick found when mothers kill their kids, 68 percent are sent to mental hospitals and 27 percent are sent to prison. When fathers kill their children, 72 percent go to prison, according to Resnick's study, and 14 percent are hospitalized.

Should we feel sorry for women who kill their children? Are they "bad" women, or does their behavior more nearly resemble that of female animals who cannot care for their young?

Once, I had the pleasure of keeping company with a cat named "Durga-Kitty." Durga-Kitty adopted Slate Branch Ashram as a place to give birth to her first litter of kitties. When her brood arrived, Durga-Kitty sent me a signal by whining softly from her maternity ward beneath the front porch. Then, she proceeded to bring all the kitties, one by one, into the house and place them lovingly in the guest bed upstairs. She used a pillow slip as an incubator for her runt.

The runt most likely would not survive, Durga-Kitty determined by a process known only to felines, so she tried to kill the little cat by pushing it aside. As her guardian, I tried to instill a super-ego into the mother of these little beings who looked more like mice, but Durga-Kitty would not abide by my rules. I would find the runt and put it back in the litter, and Durga-Kitty would cast it aside. Usually a very friendly cat, Durga-Kitty got mad when I tried to insert human ethics into her law of the wild. Rather than purring, she growled. After several days of struggle, I found the runt dead in the back of a shed behind Slate Branch House. Durga-Kitty had rejected it from the litter.

Was Durga-Kitty a "bad" mother? No, quite to the contrary, her mothering was a joy to behold. Constantly present for her babies, she gave of herself completely. But, she knew her runt would not live, I think, so she brought motherly mercy to bear on the life of the little cat who was too weak to live.

While Durga-Kitty's behavior is by no means characteristic of all human mothers, it asks us to examine maternal motivation over and beyond preconceptions of "good" and "bad."

John Jonchuck, Jr. threw his five-year-old daughter Phoebe Jade off the Sunshine Skyway Bridge in St. Petersburg, Florida on Jan. 5, 2015. Determined to be mentally unfit, he did not stand trial for his child's death by drowning. His pattern is closer to the women in Resnick's study.

Should we feel sorry for Jon Jonchuck, Jr.? Some

people might be inclined to feel even sorrier for his psychiatrist. Jonchuck might be "among those killers who cannot get forgiveness," a woman I know said. And yet, photographs of Jonchuck show a pitiful man, clearly disturbed. As human beings, should we write Jonchuck off as unforgivable?

I was living in Atlanta when the child murders happened from Summer 1979 until Spring 1981. A splash off the Chattahoochee signaled the end of a long, stressful period for the city. Police spotted a white Chevy driven by Wayne Williams on the bridge. When Williams was arrested, the killings stopped.

The Atlanta child murders, or the missing and murdered children's case, as it came to be called locally, held the city in its grip for nearly two years. At least 28 African-American children, adolescents, and adults were murdered. Williams, 23 at the time of the last killing, was convicted of the adult murders. He was suspected of the child and adolescent killings as well, but evidence was inconclusive. Williams is serving two life sentences in Georgia's Hancock State Prison in Sparta.

Should anyone feel sorry for Wayne Williams? He still maintains his innocence.

Bless their kind hearts, a number of musicians performed in Atlanta to raise money for the victims' families. Performers included Frank Sinatra, Sammy Davis, Jr., The Jacksons, and Gladys Knight and the Pips. When accepting the Best Actor Oscar for his role in "Raging Bull," Robert De Niro wore a green ribbon as a sign of solidarity with the murdered children of Atlanta.

Perhaps we all should wear green ribbons to indicate our appreciation for all the victims whose lives have been terminated abruptly. As of Dec. 2015, the third anniversary of the Sandy Hook shootings, the list was growing: children, adolescents, adults of all races and ethnicities, Whites in suburban California, Black men in midwestern cities shot by police, not by Wayne Williams.

When the murders happened in Atlanta, I was living in Grant Park not far from Memorial Drive where the children were going missing. A strange feeling settled over the city each evening. After a day's work at Emory—I was in graduate school then, also teaching some in the Graduate Institute of the Liberal Arts and the Department of English—I drove my white Chevy Malibu slowly through Cabbagetown, thinking, "I wish I could get that son-of-a-bitch and put a stop to this madness."

As a swami now, it doesn't feel good to me to write that line, but it is honestly the way I felt about the killer of Atlanta's children. At the time, I was sharing a house with a two-year-old named Zach and his mother Callahan, an artist who co-founded the Atlanta Women's Art Collective, and I feared for his safety as for other children in the city.

Anyone who has ever loved a child must surely be concerned about the question of killing as it may or may not relate to abortion. While this text does not specifically concern itself with the topic, each of us should think the matter through carefully and determine, according to our own conscience, where we stand. Another Atlanta friend named Ruthie, now an attorney in Brevard, NC, gave me a book which helped to clarify my thinking. Oriana Fallaci's *Letter to a Child Never Born* examines both sides of the abortion argument in unbiased ways. It is a model of clear thinking and good writing.

At Parliament proceedings in Salt Lake City, I felt considerable resonance with a Buddhist monk who clearly understood what I meant by "othering" human beings, victims and killers alike. John Colatch, Allegheny chaplain, now at Bucknell, turned up for my session, and it was good to see a former colleague. I know he understood. We were both in residence at Allegheny during the years after I spearheaded efforts to persuade the college to divest from companies doing business in South Africa and worked with 11 other faculty, both gay and straight, to formulate a lesbian and gay studies minor. An ordained United Methodist minister, John wrote his dissertation at Colgate Rochester Crozer on "Welcoming the Stranger" or practicing hospitality in relation to gay and lesbian people.

After many community meetings with Trustees present, Allegheny did divest, and the lesbigay minor passed unanimously on the faculty floor. We held a conference on campus called "History and Memory: Gay and Lesbian Literature Since World War II," and I edited a collection of essays based on conference proceedings for *The Journal of Homosexuality,* and as a book-length text for the Haworth Press. In the mid 1990s, *The JH* was presided over by Dr. John DeCecco, now in his late 80s and still doing activist work. DeCecco wrote a letter letting us know he was an Allegheny graduate in addition to being a gay activist. We were happy to have such a pioneer in the midst of the Allegheny family. His course called "Variations in Sexuality" drew up to 700 students each time it was offered at San Francisco State.

Turning human beings into card board figures by "othering" is not limited to sexual orientation although gay and lesbian people certainly bore the brunt of it for too long. It was my distinct honor to marry the first gay couple in Pulaski Co., Kentucky when they applied for a marriage license shortly after the historic Supreme Court decision was handed down on June 26, 2015.

Similarly, stamping "murderer" or "terrorist" on anyone's brow is not likely to halt either the purchase of assault rifles or the construction of bombs. When we "other" human beings and fail to take them seriously, they often strike back. Either that, or they turn the anger inward, and in time, the rage turns into resentment strong enough to take down the World Trade Towers—or create a revolution.

"Othering" can be subtle. In his CNN newscast on Dec. 10, 2015, Jake Tapper referred to Jihadist conversations on the Internet as "chatter." How might Tapper feel, I wonder, if a Jihadist called his reporting "babble" or "prattle?" As it turns out, Tashfeen Malik had been "chattering" on Social Media for a couple of years about wanting to commit jihad before she finally did it.

Do I feel sorry for Tashfeen Malik? Yes, definitely. Tashfeen Malik broke my heart. I understand her religious perspective, I think, but the feminist in me wants to reach out across the grave and say, "Tashfeen, dear one, women should know better than to pledge allegiance to a male authority figure who encourages violence."

A problem with "othering" people, or taking them out, whatever our justification, is that we do not know how close they may be to making a change for the better. As it did with John Lennon, the light can switch on quickly when it seems to be nowhere in sight. Transformation can be closer than the breath.

Should we feel sorry for killers who have outlived their victims? Truman Capote did, and he wrote a bestseller entitled *In Cold Blood*. Would Dick Hickok and Perry Smith, the killers in Capote's book, have been candidates for transformation had they not been hanged for multiple murders committed in a small Kansas town?

In Cold Blood was first published in 1966, and it instantly became a bestseller. Capote's is the second biggest best selling true crime title in publishing history behind Vincent Bugliosi's *Helter Skelter,* about the Charles Manson murders, published in 1974.

Pity may be "condescending," as Sally Fitzgerald once said over lunch in Atlanta during one of our many intense conversations, but it is a step closer to compassion than is sentimentality. Compassion is rendered by no judgment at all—very difficult in a society which consistently confuses the judgmental capacity with the critical intellect.

CHAPTER IV

THREE BIG TIME KILLERS TRANSFORMED

We often use the word "killer" as if it were hard-wired in our bodies, an indelible entry in our ethical thesaurus. Other criminals can be cured, given good doctors and appropriate medications, we seem to think, but "killers are killers," and it is probably best to keep them out of harm's way. Our attitude toward killers is reflected in the language we speak, in our projections: "We better not let that killer out of jail—he might kill again."

Some fairly strong evidence suggests otherwise. Take, for instance, the transformation of three big time killers.

Saul (first century, CE) was a murderer of Christians. He had a dramatic conversion experience when he was blinded by the light of the road to Damascus, historically an Islamic caliphate base for a time, now in war torn Syria. According to Acts 9 of the Christian Bible, Jesus spoke to Saul from afar, and when the scales fell off his eyes, he could see again. He took the name Paul and stopped killing Christians even though Jews kept trying to kill him.

Milarepa (1052-1135), or Jetson Milarepa, is considered to be one of Tibet's most accomplished yogis and poets. In his daily life, prior to awakening, he was a sorcerer who killed by summoning hail storms and demolishing villages. He finally convinced Marpa, a great spiritual master, to teach him meditation. When he learned how to be still, his interior life changed. He altered his ways and began using his psychic gifts to help the very people he had once murdered by using black magic. Were Milarepa alive today, he might be effective in teaching the Chinese how to meditate and respect Tibetan culture.

"The Uttara Kanda," the last seven books of the *Ramayana* written sometime between the first and fifth centuries, BCE, recounts the story of Valmiki's early life as Ratnakar, a highway robber who killed after stealing people blind. Ratnakar made the mistake of attempting to rob the sage Narada who managed to turn his thinking inside out. Ratnakar became Valmiki, penned the epic *Ramayana*, in part his autobiography, and became *Adi Kavi*, the first poet in Sanskrit. No mean achievement for an Indian crook who undoubtedly could have helped to thwart the 12 attacks on Mumbai extending over a four day period in 2008.

These three men from the history of the world's religions were notorious killers. Had they been extinguished, the religions they represent would be seriously diminished.

The state of California has been experimenting with the rehabilitation of killers with considerable success. In her book entitled *Life After Murder: Five Men in Search of Redemption*, Nancy Mullane explores the question: Can killers ever be transformed?

Mullane made several trips to California's San Quentin Prison to interview convicts who were locked up for murder. Jesse Reed, one of the men profiled in her book, was sentenced to 27 years to life and later paroled.

Reed told Mullane he had no intention of taking the life of a man he attempted to rob, but he needed money on the spot to buy drugs, so he wound up shooting Joseph Bates.

"When you're nervous, you're not really thinking clear," Reed said. "Today I'm an individual who decided that he really wanted to change. Change comes from within. It's just having a desire to be better."

According to Mullane, as cited by NPR's Scott Simon, from 1990 until May 31, 2011, about 1,000 individuals who were serving sentences for first or second degree murder were paroled from California prisons. Of that 1,000, zero have killed again.

These are convincing statistics. But, are they compelling enough to persuade us to think twice before cringing fearfully in the presence of a former killer?

I once met a man named Thomas Ambrose Toomey (1923-2006) who went into prisons to teach meditation. In a sense, Tom Toomey was doing what Marpa did with Milarepa, and what Narada did with Valmiki. Tom Toomey died of natural causes, and his memory serves as a testament to how business in prisons could be conducted more humanely.

Would Tom Toomey have gone into the Federal Supermax Prison in Florence, Colorado to teach Dzhokhar, the younger of the Tsarnaev brothers responsible for the Boston Marathon Bombings, killing three and wounding 260, how to meditate?

The Boston Marathon is held on Patriot's Day commemorating the battles that launched the American Revolution at Lexington and Concord where a total of 122 colonists and British were killed, 213 wounded. The course is 26.2 miles long. The Tsarnaev brothers disrupted the distinctly American celebration on April 15, 2013, also tax day.

After the bombings, his brother dead, Dzhokhar was found in a 24-foot dry-docked boat in Watertown, Massachusetts. He had scrawled a note saying the Boston Marathon bombings were committed in retaliation for U.S. wars in Muslim countries. His note didn't mention wanting to appear on the cover of *Rolling Stone*.

Dzhokhar Tsarnaev became an American citizen on Sept. 11, 2012, the eleventh anniversary of the World Trade Towers disaster.

I cannot say for certain, but I think Tom Toomey would have wanted to offer Dzhokhar Tsarnaev a chance at redemption. Toomey was a former Dominican father, and I suspect he might have said, with the Anglican poet-priest John Donne, "any man's death diminishes me."

Question is: Would Dzhokhar Tsarnaev want a shot at becoming a big time killer transformed? At being remembered as a Saul, Milarepa, or Valmiki instead of a little brother who went along for the ride? In his mind, what is redemption when compared to martyrdom?

CHAPTER V

THEY ARE MUSLIMS, TOO

Over and again, in the wake of the San Bernardino Massacre, we heard ongoing denouncements to the effect that the Jihadists are not full-fledged Muslims. It is pointless to cite speakers and dates. The litany was always the same. The Jihadists are not true Muslims.

Even Karen Armstrong in her erudition makes a similar point in *Fields of Blood*. The Jihadists are not authentic Muslims, Armstrong says. Many are thugs, and some got their religion from *Islam for Dummies*.

Make no mistake. I do not support jihad, or any form of violence. But, the Jihadists are Muslims, too. In fact, they may be truer to the religion practiced by Muhammad than many Western Muslims are with their modern attitudes.

The Prophet was fierce and aggressive, as much a military man as an imam. He invented the surprise attack, Armstrong says, and he killed his own followers when it suited his purposes. Known to raid tribes outside Medina, he eventually marched on Mecca. He didn't amble in, prayer beads in hand, peace mantras on his lips.

Religions operate along a continuum from orthodox and fundamentalist to reformed. In taking the *Quran* literally, the Jihadists appeal to some 109 passages in which Muhammad instructs Muslims to kill the Heathen. The Prophet was intent on building a Muslim nation much as the Jihadists want to build an Islamic state. And, he succeeded. The Umayyad (and later the Abbasid) Muslim empires once stretched across Eurasia from Saudi Arabia to Spain.

As Michael Weiss and Hassan Hassan note, when

the notorious Abu Musab al-Zarqawi turned to drink and crime, his mother enrolled him in a religious school to sober him up. At the Al-Husayn Ben Ali Mosque in Amman, al-Zarqawi discovered Salafism, a doctrine which, in its contemporary form, advocates a return to theological purity and the traditions of the prophet Muhammad.

Salafists deem Western-style democracy and modernity not only "fundamentally irreconcilable with Islam," Weiss and Hassan write, "but the main pollutants" of Arab civilization. At the most extreme end of the continuum, the Salafists are also adherents of jihad as was al-Zarqawi in his role as leader of al-Qaeda in Iraq from 2004-2006.

At the reformed end of the spectrum, Muslims exercise more liberty to pick and choose their Quarnic interpretations and practices. While many are unquestionably devout, they do not scour their sacred scripture in search of justifications for killing the Infidel, even though they may oppose American involvement in the Middle East. In a word, they are assimilated into Western culture and have no wish to return to their countries of origin or to the desert with few modern conveniences. Many travel to visit relatives, but they return to lives much like any other American citizen.

Donald Trump's press release stating that he, Donald J. Trump, would ban Muslims from entering the United States until U.S. representatives figured out "what the hell" they are doing set off a firestorm among journalists as well as international Muslims in the moderate camp.

Chris Cuomo got so rattled on CNN's "New Day" that he talked over Trump when "the Donald" was trying to explain his position. Eyes blazing, Cuomo started with an agenda rather than asking questions in time-honored journalistic fashion. Ironically, he bullied Trump. Usually, it is Donald Trump who reflects a sensibility closer to the last of the great Prophets.

Why any orthodox or reformed Muslim, or journalist leaning to the left or right would get excited over Trump's pronouncements is beyond a good many people, supporters and detractors alike, who are onto his strategies. As John King, CNN senior political analyst for CNN, said shortly after Trump wrote the Ban Muslim headline for all the world to read, "Trump knows what he is doing. He knows his audience."

Indeed, Donald Trump knows how to rally his troops. By using a triumphant brand of overstatement and unapologetic insult, Trump strikes at the heart of a populous who is genuinely worried for its own security. As Trump himself said, "those weren't Swedes who knocked down the World Trade Towers."

Of course, Trump would be concerned about the towers as he has constructed a number of tall buildings himself. But, his ability to capitalize on the fever of the moment has as much to do with journalistic presentation and viewer reception as it does with a talent for inciting heated reactions.

In the United States, post San Bernardino Massacre, the liberal contingent appears to be as protective of Muslims in Michigan as of Jews in Israel. In the sense that Muslims in the West know how to make money and form an affluent community respectful of the American Dream, they are in a position much like Jewish people were earlier. Of course, American Muslims are generous, too, and they give to their communities. Generosity is a mandate in Islam.

Make no mistake. I would have a great deal of

difficulty voting for Donald Trump should he get the Republication nomination or run independently for President. I have voted for every Yellow Dog Democrat who has run—and won or gotten clobbered—since I was granted the right to vote in my home state of Kentucky. One of my most treasured possessions is a letter from Senator Edmund Muskie (D-MAINE) saying he shared my opinion "that the war must end now and that we must never again have another Vietnam."

Happily, it was Kentucky's own Sen. John Sherman Cooper, a moderate Republican, who introduced the amendment to bring American troops home from southeast Asia. Cooper was an old-school statesman, the bipartisan kind who knew how to reach across the aisle and elicit cooperation from Democrats. In an age of divisive and dualistic politics, we don't see many John Sherman Coopers any more.

At Christmas one year when we were in high school, Cooper's sister-in-law Cornelia gave a holiday party for her daughter Neil. Sen. Cooper was present. Every young woman who wanted to got to dance with the Senator who treated each of us with decorum and respect. Graciousness may be out-dated, but civility helps to create a climate of peace as well as workable relations among our elected officials.

Sen. Cooper also hosted our high school band in the nation's capital when we traveled to New York City to march in the Macy's Day Parade in 1962. We took a train from Somerset to Washington, D.C. where Sen. Cooper met and treated us to lunch. From D.C., we traveled to NYC by bus, and it was a great trip. It was fun zooming in through the Lincoln Tunnel and seeing the city for the first time. Little did I know then, even before the Beatles invaded America, that I would have a long lasting relationship with New York that stretches into the present.

Somerset, Kentucky, where both Sen. John Sherman Cooper and I grew up and graduated from Somerset High School, is located on the buckle of the Bible Belt in fundamentalist Christian territory. More than 90 Baptist churches grace these rolling hills. Since Somerset has become a medical center, a cadre of Muslim doctors has migrated here and opened up shop. They have built a small mosque that sits quietly on a side street not far from Lake Cumberland.

It would never occur to me, or to most anyone who lives here, to think of the major religion that is practiced in these parts as being less Christian that the liberal variety espoused by theologian Dr. John Killinger, also a graduate of Somerset High School. Individuals ranging from the cerebral theologian Paul Tillich who escaped from Nazi Germany to passionate Jerry Falwell, spokesman for the Religious Right as well as Killinger's nemesis, are both Christian. Neither is more or less Christian than the other. Both practice authentic forms of the faith handed down by apostles across the centuries.

Jihad is the sticking point, isn't it? Modern Muslims seek to distance themselves from bombings and machine gun assaults just as many Christians want no part of snake handling or speaking in tongues. Certain practices are too dangerous for inclusion in a reformed agenda, whether Christian or Muslim. Tell a snake handler to put away his copperheads and sit in church like a good deacon, and he most likely will turn the poison in your direction. Tell a Jihadist to put away his bombs, and expect an explosion on your doorstep.

After the Paris attacks, I emailed a Muslim friend, a

French woman who lives in Somerset with her husband, a Muslim doctor from Egypt, and their children. I wanted my friend to know I was thinking of her and others at the mosque who are integral parts of our town. My friend emailed back with an invitation to attend a program at the mosque, a memorial service for those killed in Paris.

While sitting at the mosque, listening to Pat express surprise that any Muslim would engage in violence like that displayed in Paris, I remembered a night at Professors Laura and Leo Weddle's home when Leo charged out of his library bearing a copy of the *Quran*.

"I found this in a thrift store," Leo said. "It is inscribed to one of the local churches downtown."

When I told my Muslim friend about this wayward copy of the *Quran*, she was kind enough to suggest someone might have "recycled" it. Her interpretation was, perhaps, more generous than deserved.

A Jihadist most likely would claim that disposing of the *Quran*, the sacred scripture of Islam, is an act of violence. Whether or not the Jihadist would seek revenge, however, would depend on a number of mitigating factors, including whether or not it is his or her time to throw the proverbial prayer shawl into the fire leading to martyrdom.

"There will be wars and rumors of war," the Christian Bible says. America finally got out of Vietnam, but it was not long before President George W. Bush invaded Iraq purportedly looking for weapons of mass destruction. I did not support Bush's policy then, and American spiritual leader Marianne Williamson calls it disastrous.

Whether we like it or not, America has had a hand in helping the Jihadists get their start. From Sept. 1, 2001 forward, we have been feeling the effects of a cultural clash sometimes labeled a Holy War. In my view, there is nothing sacred about killing. But, killing is part of the Jihadist worldview.

And, the Jihadists are Muslims, too.

CHAPTER VI

THE HISTORY OF KILLING

In the wake of the latest mass murder, we may be inclined to think of killing as something new, a product of modern confusion, perhaps, or the inevitable result of life after the Holocaust. Actually, killing has been with us longer than anyone would care to remember.

We are beginning to piece together a timeline of killing from evidence gathered by scientists. A 2013 discovery in Spain led a research team to theorize that murder may pre-date human society. The team stumbled upon 30 skulls they dated back to the middle of the Pleistocene era around 430,000 years ago. One skull showed evidence of blunt force to the head and may belong to the first human murdered on earth, scientists said.

Whether or not the skeletons found inside the Spanish cave dubbed *Sima de los Huesos,* or "Pit of Bones," represent the first mass murder in human history is open to question. If these 30 bodies were dropped into the cave via a shaft, it is possible to conclude they may have been someone's victims—or someone's sacrifice. If early humans were living in the cave as a dwelling, then the fractures on one skull may point to a skirmish of some kind. If the fracture is evidence of murder, it is somewhat hopeful to think the murder may have taken place a long time after the first humans allegedly appeared in Africa some five to seven million years ago. Of course, we don't know what else scientists might find in unexplored caverns beneath the earth in Spain, Africa, or Kentucky for that matter, where caves are abundant.

Maybe these skulls belonged to the tribe of Cain and Abel. In the Christian world, the death of Abel is frequently cited as the world's first murder, but we do not really know where Cain and Abel lived, where Cain murdered his brother, or if they were flesh and blood men in addition to being mythic constructions. The chapter of "Genesis" tells us Eve gave birth to these boys, and then Cain attacked his brother in the fields. Maybe the setting was located in Spain near *Sima de Los Heusos,* but Biblical scholars tend to think the family of Adam and Eve appeared somewhere in the Middle East, possibly in or near what is now Syria.

Do the *Vedas,* the oldest Indian scriptures, mention killing? According to the *Athara Veda* 10.1.29, it is a great sin to kill innocent cows, horses, and people. Killing is clearly prohibited in the *Vedas.* Since the *Vedas* pre-date the chapter of "Genesis" by several thousand years, perhaps the skulls found in the "Pit of Bones" belong to the Aryans who invaded north India. Then again, scholars tend to think the Aryans came to India from the steppes of Russia.

How little we know scientifically about the beginnings and migration patterns of the human race, much less the history of killing. From the literature and drama of our race, however, we certainly can discern that killing claims a substantial number of pages in our book of life. The great epics of both East and West focus intensely on killing.

For several years after taking early retirement from Allegheny College, I taught *The Mahabharata* alongside *The Odyssey* and *The Iliad* in the Honors Program curriculum at the University of Kentucky. Most faculty dealt with the Greeks alone, but as a comparatist with a special interest in India, I chose to juxtapose the classics from both hemispheres.

All three focus on killing. All three deal with war and death. Thus, we could say that killing is a cornerstone in the history of Eastern and Western literature.

One semester, I focused on the plays of William Shakespeare. The blood in the bard's tragedies is enough to sink the island of Great Britain.

Like Krzysztof Kieslowski, William Shakespeare got inside his characters who are always three-dimensional. Like Kieslowski, Shakespeare was interested in ethical violations. Who among us is likely to forget the blood Macbeth managed to spill as a result of his vaulting ambition? So close, at least metaphorically, to the economic meltdown on Wall St. in 2008. Although considerably more dramatic, Shakespeare is no less an ethicist than Kieslowski.

My encounter with William Shakespeare goes back to childhood. My mother read a simplified version of *Macbeth* (and *The Odyssey*) to me not too long after I could walk. Before I entered formal schooling at age five, I could do my multiplication tables and recite poetry outloud, thanks to my educator mother. It's no wonder I wound up being a professor, a professional student, one whose Ph.D. was painless. That old schoolgirl game seems to have come in with me on my genes, and my mother recognized me for who I was and would grow up to be.

I won't belabor the issue of past lives and *karma* in relation to killing—it is far too complicated to take on in a short book. While the idea of we "reap what we sow " stands to reason, many of the killings post 9/11, and during 9/11 itself, seem to suggest that the law of *karma* may have broken down in postmodern times. If the law of *dharma* can go underground, then why not the law of *karma*? It is difficult to grasp, but the law of *karma* does say a cause-effect relationship exists in everything that happens.

Are we to believe all the people killed on 9/11 somehow brutalized the Jihadists in a former life? Maybe during the Crusades? Do we seriously accept Mark David Chapman as a figure from John Lennon's past lives? His jilted lover, perhaps, in the days when they hung out with Oscar Wilde and Lord Alfred Douglas? Were the 14 people killed in the San Bernardino Massacre standing in a room in southern California waiting to receive their karmic comeuppance?

The answer would be yes—well, I guess it might be yes—within the context of a certain Western tendency to extrapolate meaning in terms of relationships and *karma*. It may be wise, however, to heed the Buddhist caution and take care not to get overly invested in the narratives we construct to make life—and death—more interesting.

In 6th grade, I gave a book report on "Macbeth," and the teacher gave me a C. She probably did not believe I had read Shakespeare's play; either that, or she feared I might put murderous ideas into the heads of my colleagues. In those days, we didn't have violent video games. We watched "Fury," the story of a hero stallion, on Saturday morning TV. Eventually, I forgave my teacher, now deceased, for her failure to recognize my keen literary critical ability, as I wanted to spare her karmically. But, I think it might be a good idea for middle school teachers now to deal with killing as the serious problem it is in postmodern culture. In some schools, Columbine, Colorado and Sandy Hook, Connecticut, for instance, teachers and students have had no choice but to confront the problem of killing upfront.

Often, in the West, we tend to think of East and West as if there were no in between. In reality, however, the Middle East also produced an epic of equal stature. *One Thousand and One Nights,* compiled in Arabic during the Islamic "Golden Age," features the same epic characteristics we find in Homer and Vyasa. The "Golden Age" spans five centuries from the 8th to the 13th under the Abbasid Dynasty when Islamic culture became a blending of Arab, Persian, Egyptian, and European traditions. The result, according to some scholars, was a "stunning" era of intellectual and cultural achievement although the Crusades were in full tilt about the middle of this time period from the 10th to the 12th centuries.

Parts of *One Thousand and One Nights,* or *The Arabian Nights* as these tales are known in the West, are not included in the original Arabic version. Scholars think "Aladdin's Wonderful Lamp," "Ali Baba and the Forty Thieves," and "The Seven Voyages of Sinbad the Sailor" may have been added to the collection by Antoine Galland and other European translators.

From Persia comes the *Shahnameh,* "The Book of Kings" in 60,000 verses. This text begins in pre-Islamic Iran in the mythic times of creation and closes with the Arab-Muslim conquest. The translation by Dick Davis, who is thought to be the best translator of this Persian epic, was called "violent and beautiful" by a major American newspaper.

The combination of these adjectives, "violent and beautiful," says much about all the epics constructed by the human race to date. Whether we are Western, Eastern, or Middle Eastern, is it possible to imagine a beautiful epic with no violence? Lest we not forget Dante's *The Divine Comedy*, a long Christian poem, circa 1300, written in *terza rima.* Murderers and suicides appear in Canto 7 near the bottom of Dante's "Inferno."

The late Prof. Arthur Evans, with whom I took a two-semester seminar in *The Divine Comedy* at Emory, was attentive to the ethical dimensions of Dante's poem. And, when my time came to offer an in-class presentation, I chose Canto 1 of "The Purgatorio." Here, Dante pilgrim emerges from Hell on Easter morning , and it is the virtue of humility which allows him to begin his climb up through Purgatory and into Paradise.

Arthur Evans was one of the most extraordinary beings I have ever encountered. Long before anyone began to speak of ISIS or radical Islam, Arthur was interested in the relationship between mysticism and terrorism. For certain, mysticism without discipline and the rational faculty which keeps far flung fantasies in check can result in impulses which tend to overtake the ethical capacity.

At Allegheny, when I directed the Humanities Core, we offered a three-semester course in which contemporary works of art, music, and literature were keyed to Hell, Purgatory, and Paradise as states of consciousness. The course was dedicated to Arthur Evans. Class discussion was astonishing.

In the 1990s, we offered a version of the Dante sequence, coupled with the *Ramayana,* to a small group of students being educated inside my Guru's ashram. When these dear ones applied to go out to boarding school, the headmaster where some of the older ones were accepted was very pleased with their training. I was not surprised to see them accepted to a good school since studying two epics in comparison with each other—and in relation to their own spiritual practice—must have contributed enormously to their intellectual attainment.

I would like to see a similar educational experience offered to students across the United States beginning in First Grade. Given exposure to both Satan and Ratnakar, it would be difficult for students to glorify the paper thin gangsters of video game violence considered within the context of the monstrous creatures in the great epics who are far more instructive.

If students come from atheist homes, no problem. All the great epics can be read as mythical texts which offer life lessons. There is so much war in *The Iliad,* for example, that peace becomes an attractive option. *The Odyssey* has not been rivaled for its presentation of the journey motif. In many ways, the story of Odysseus is our own.

As we come forward in time, the focus on killing escalates exponentially, especially in the movies. So much so that Oliver Stone reportedly spent a mere $34,000,000 to make an allegedly satiric film about killing called "Natural Born Killers" (referred to previously). Although Stone's film was said to be satire, it may have had another effect. It has been theorized that "Natural Born Killers" was the inspiration for the Columbine killings.

Again, we come up against the problem of complicity. While it is a given that actors, as well as journalists, must work for a living, professionals do have some say-so over the contracts they choose to sign. While "Natural Born Killers" propelled Woody Harrelson to the top of the charts, we have to ask if the film's box office results of $50.3 million and the fame it produced for Harrelson were worth the harm the movie may have caused others.

When compared to the meager $100,000 spent to make all the parts of "The Decalogue," now an undisputed classic, the figures for "Natural Born Killers" seem to be somewhat extravagant, don't they?

Where are the films produced in Hollywood which inveigh against killing? "Pulp Fiction" (1994) does not seem to fall into this category, but it could be argued the film's black humor ultimately provides a critique of violence.

"Saving Private Ryan" (1998) is a realistic portrayal of war, hard to take, but it undoubtedly deserves to be on the National Film Registry for its depiction of the Invasion of Normandy in World War II. "Coming Home" (1978) had much to say about the pain of Vietnam while garnering Academy Awards for John Voigt and Jane Fonda in the lead roles. "Johnny Got His Gun" (1971), based on a 1938 anti-war novel by Dalton Trumbo, has become something of a cult film and is guaranteed to haunt as viewers witness a fallen soldier, an amputee unable to speak, trying to peck out the words, "please kill me."

"American Sniper" and "13 Hours" are certainly not in the running for Best Picture That Inveighs Against Killing. Both glorify the iconic gun and move it more deeply into the psyche as a powerful symbol of destruction. "13 Hours" is a natural choice for viewers who are titillated by explosions.

"Schindler's List" (1993) is a clear winner here. The story of Oskar Schindler, a German industrialist who managed to save the lives of about 1,200 Jews by employing them in a munitions factory, "Schindler's List" is generally considered to be Steven Spielberg's masterpiece. In my view, this film comes close to Kieslowski's "A Short Film about Killing" in terms of sincerity. Sincerity is hard to find in the postmodern age which is known for its ability to turn almost anything into a joke—ultimately, the failure of "Natural Born Killers."

I would like to nominate Oskar Schindler for a honorary Oscar (please do not laugh at the incidental word play, or put this recommendation in Anderson's Cooper's "Ridiculist" suggestion box). May Schindler be placed in the company of Saul, Milarepa, and Valmiki for his contribution to a less brutal world.

When war turned global, the representation of killing became less heroic than it was in ancient Greece, India, and Arabia. With the loss of the heroic in literature and drama, an anti-hero emerged. The anti-hero kills without conscience. He is personified by Jacek in Kieslowski's "A Short Film about Killing." He always has the freedom to kill, not just when he is being tested existentially as was the case with Ernest Hemingway's protagonists, according to John Killinger's *Hemingway and the Dead Gods.*

If the gods are dead, then what is human being's reason for living? Our very lack of purpose, or what Indians call *dharma,* may be a major reason for killing in contemporary times whereas the ancients killed on purpose—to survive, defend their tribes, advance their holdings. In this respect, ISIS comes closer to killing with purpose than most of the mass killers who were raised on Western alienation.

Written sometime between 1100 and 400 BCE, we think, a section of *The Mahabharata, The Bhagavad Gita,* may tell us as much about killing as all the carnage in Karen Armstrong's *Fields of Blood.* Not to diminish Armstrong's book—it makes an important contribution to the history of killing at a time when such an exploration is very much needed. *Fields of Blood* is a formal history, and we need to know where we have been to figure out where we are going. *Fields of Blood* may well help lead us toward a paradigm of non harming.

Are we capable of living in a world in which killing is no longer an option? If so, how might we arrive at such a place where the old paradigm of war and death gives way to a more spacious landscape? If we are willing to question even Krishna, the god in our chariot, when he urges us to kill our cousins on the battlefield of life; if we are willing to allow the findings of science, the social sciences, and the humanities to act as partners; if we can see our way clear to putting some trust in David Sloan Wilson's research, we might even wind up thinking that altruism is possible because of our genetic makeup. If we've had enough of selfishness, we may be willing to evolve beyond the "selfish gene."

Of course, Vyasa, author of *The Mahabharata* from which *The Bhagavad Gita* is excerpted, knew Arjuna would wax philosophical when Krishna taunted him with the idea of killing his brothers. Either that, or Arjuna's not wanting to fight reflected the sensibility of a natural born pacifist, a lamb in sheep's clothing trying to masquerade as a wolf.

The British director Peter Brook made a film of *The Mahabharata* (1989) based on his 1985 stage play which lasted nine hours. Brook did a great job of assembling a multicultural cast, but predictably, certain critics objected. When Brook cut the play down to three hours for filmic consumption, length was still a problem for many viewers accustomed to sound bytes. Also, Brook's filmic adaptation was released during the so-called "cultural wars" in academe when Professor Stanley Fish was known to get into fist fights. Too bad Kieslowski is not still alive to bring his minimalist touch to Brook's not inconsiderable efforts. Kieslowski most likely could edit *The Mahabharata* down to a series resembling "The Decalogue" and not lose an ounce of its integrity.

Or, perhaps, flesh out the story of those 30 skulls found in a cave in Spain.

CHAPTER VII

KILLING AS REALITY TV

There's so much killing on television these days that it is becoming increasingly hard to tell news from drama. If I didn't know better, I might think CNN's "New Day" is a dramatic show as opposed to a platform for the morning news. On the other hand, many of the dramatic shows on television have gotten so flat and predictable they resemble what we used to call news. There's more drama on "New Day" now than there is on "Law and Order."

Recently, I performed a little experiment. "I bet I can turn the TV on at random," I thought, "and there will be no mention of killing." Wrong. An advertisement was on, and the first word out of the actor's mouth was, "kill." As the southern writer Flannery O'Connor once asked, who speaks for America today? Her answer: Madison Ave. Madison Ave. taps into the unconscious layers, what Sigmund Freud called the id, where fears and dreams are made. Madison Ave. shows us what we are really thinking about down deep.

In my humble opinion, it should not be in the least mysterious as to why we see so many killings now. In reality, I mean. The airways are saturated with killings, and the only way to keep the killings out of consciousness is to turn the TV or computer off. Even then, there's no guarantee. Vibrations in consciousness have a way of seeping into individual minds, and letting us know where the next killing might occur.

"Violent crime has been steadily declining across America," said President Obama during "Guns in America" on CNN, "but you wouldn't know it by watching television."

When I trained journalists at Allegheny College, as part of a generalist position which included teaching literature and interdisciplinary studies, I taught students to distinguish between hard news and opinion/editorial. Students learned to live and die by the Sigma Delta Chi Code of Ethics for journalists. I took this job, because I had worked as a journalist/editor in Atlanta, and I wanted to hang my hat at a good liberal arts college with a reputation for academic rigor. The journalistic assignment kept me in touch with the heart beat of the campus.

The heat started the day I arrived from Atlanta in September 1982. The editor, a dedicated guy named Billy Gratin, said he had heard the college chaplain had been asked to resign for skinny dipping in the Sea of Galilee with students. As might be expected, reporters for *The Campus* newspaper couldn't get anyone on the record. So, we dropped the nameplate to three-quarters, and ran a front page banner head: "Hobson Resigns: College, No Comment." This story turned a sleepy little college newspaper into a publication that had people running to get the latest edition.

Probably the hardest year we faced was when former Republican Governor Raymond Shafer served as Interim President of the College. Governor Shafer thought college newspapers should be publicity vehicles, leaflets Trustees could hand out to prospective donors, and he was none too happy when editors made sure he got his personal copy by placing one under the windshield wipers of his car. Sometimes, when the paper came out, Andy Ford, then Dean of the College, called my office with a one-word message: "Duck."

Andy left Allegheny to become President of Wabash College, and *The Campus* newspaper changed editors every year. Never, to my knowledge, did anyone on staff overstep his or her boundaries. These student journalists were being trained professionally, and they responded in kind. As is the case for liberal arts college graduates, most went into fields other than journalism after graduation, but a few played it close to the vest of words. Arsen Kashkashian is head book buyer and general manager for the Boulder Bookstore, one of the last great independent bookstores in the United States. Chris Shipley, who went into tech writing, is said to have popularized the term, "Social Media."

We worked with all kinds of stories at Allegheny, but I always emphasized hard news as the basic building block. Granted, certain forms of new journalism tend to mix hard news and op/ed. But never, in my view, should a journalist lean so far toward op/ed that his opinion reveals itself in the questions he asks.

Carly Fiorina, candidate for the Republican presidential nomination, chastened Chris Cuomo in a "New Day" segment following the San Bernardino Massacre for bringing an agenda to his fact gathering process. Chris Cuomo snapped back, and for a moment, I thought the two were going to have an argument. The interaction resembled a scene in a daytime soap more than it did news.

In her interview with CNN's Don Lemon, Star Jones made some fascinating observations about Donald Trump. While most reporters were worrying the airwaves silly over Trump's banning Muslims from entering United States comment, Lemon seemed okay with allowing Star Jones to have her say.

Donald Trump "reminds me of Russell Crowe at the end of 'Gladiator,'" Star Jones said. "As Crowe stands tall amid death and destruction, he comments, 'Are you not entertained?'" she added.

Indeed, Trump showed himself to be a consummate entertainer when he told a crowd at a Christian college in Iowa: "I could stand in the middle of Fifth Avenue and shoot somebody, and I wouldn't lose any voters, OK?" The audience laughed.

Perhaps our need to be entertained helps to keep the killings in motion. If we are thrilled by watching people wiped out, or hearing about it in retrospect, what does this say about us as a human race? Are our lives so boring we must seek stimulation in celluloid killings? Is the news so mundane that producers and reporters must give it some spice to compete with reality TV, and in the process, jack up their ratings?

By his own admission, Donald Trump is an entertainer. To many folks across our land, his acting translates as: "Trump is his own man. Nobody can buy him." If he isn't elected President of the United States, Donald Trump could produce a news show, or become a news commentator himself. He would do well in pivotal slots. But, why should he bother? He already has prime time in his back pocket.

To his credit, when the sheriff in Roseburg, Oregon declined to name the killer at Umpqua Community College, Don Lemon said, "it's our job" to answer the questions which make the news—the Who, What, Where, When, Why and How related to a story. Without the killer's name, the story would have been seriously incomplete.

And, yet, killers seem to be increasingly interested in celebrity. The Roseburg, Oregon killer said as much. He even smiled before he opened fire, presumably so the video camera would capture his rise to stardom. In a note he left on the bloody scene, he mentioned killers being in the "limelight."

At the Parliament session in Salt Lake City, one man said, "I guarantee you, take them off TV, and the killings will stop."

It's a dilemma for news organizations. To get a complete story, the 5Ws and an H must be answered. At the same time, the killers are players in their own reality TV dramas. Perhaps not by design of the networks, news and reality TV have overlapped. Their components intermingle.

The only foolproof way I have found to be able to determine whether a TV show is news or drama is to count the number of times the gun appears during an episode. On this front, news producers tend to favor words over images. Dramatic shows, on the other hand, tend to be in love with the image of the gun—the gun as star. Framing the gun from various angles is a preoccupation among directors, it would appear.

When we turn on our TVs in the evening after work, maybe to wind down before bedtime, we find an infinity of angles on the iconic gun: closeups, fadeaways, gun barrels and fingers on triggers brought into stark relief in much the same way images are positioned in paintings. We take the gun with us into our dreams, and when we wake up, we turn on "New Day," or another show on a competing network, only to have gun-speak replace gun-see.

For this reason, The Sacred Feet Publishing Imprint has placed a photograph of the iconic gun on the cover of this book just beneath the word KILLING in all capital letters. And, still, some people will ask: Why is the A-15, "America's Gun," featured on a book written by a monk? Monks ought to stay in monasteries and renounce all things worldly, including guns and TVs. Monks ought to pray for peace rather than stick their noses into serious subjects like violence.

Fr. Thomas Merton published a book entitled *Conjectures of a Guilty Bystander*. Merton wasn't very good at letting harm go by without finding some way to address it. Neither am I. When we are constantly confronted by the damaging effects of the gun, then it is time to take an in-your-face approach. The gun is on the cover of this book, because this smoking piece of metal is an instrument of death not just on TV, not just in the movies, not just in video games.

Guns, guns, guns! In a CNN newscast on Jan. 11, 2016, both Anderson Cooper and Martin Savidge called the video highlighting Mexican drug lord El Chapo's escape through a sewage tunnel, and subsequent arrest, "extraordinary." Extraordinary, indeed—downright Dantean! The video was a shoot-em-up with lots of gunfire and no recognizable human being. More "extraordinary" was the fact that actor Sean Penn slipped into Mexico to interview El Chapo and, according to CNN, gave him editorial control of the story published in *Rolling Stone*. Anything for a sensational story, I guess, although Penn claimed in an interview with Charlie Rose for "60 Minutes" to be "really sad about the state of journalism in our country." I can see Ben Bradlee, *Washington Post* editor during the Watergate era, shaking his head in disbelief.

One of my favorite moments in "Killing as Reality TV" occurs when reporters cite ISIS as a reliable source. After the San Bernardino Massacre, commentators across the time slots wanted to know if ISIS had responded to the deadly shooting. Understandably, I suppose, reporters were wondering what home base might have to say as to whether or not the perpetrators were "official" killers. If they were "unofficial," or simply "ISIS-inspired," what might these distinctions mean?

Onto the camera came the "talking heads" who were given a few seconds to think discursively about the killings at hand. Some of the "talking heads" are "official" network commentators, and some are brought on especially to theorize in "expert" ways about matters ranging from what ISIS "might" be planning next to what might be "trending" in the moment.

When the "talking heads" arrive, I usually switch the TV off. I used to listen closely to Peter Berger's remarks, but since he has come in out of the field and joined a think tank, he strikes me as far more tame than he used to be. Michael Weiss of *The Daily Beast* provided a thought-provoking perspective in the wake of San Bernardino. Weiss is a student of Middle Eastern culture, and like many bright students, he looks away bored, if not somewhat embarrassed, by uninformed questions he is asked to answer. An uptown West Side New Yorker, he isn't easily fooled by anyone's rhetoric. If Weiss turns into a "talking head," we will know that cable news can co-opt even the most independent thinker into a candidate for daytime drama.

CNN, Dec. 8, 2015—A reporter named Alisyn Camerota was interviewing two young Muslims who resembled Syed Farook and Tashfeen Malik. The male was slightly westernized, as I recall, and the female was wearing an *hijab*, her head covered. The visual contrast between West and Middle East was more than a little striking. To an educated eye, the gap in cultural values was apparent. Also, and I am somewhat hesitant to make this remark, but I understood more fully during this telecast why we Westerners, caught up in appearances, look like Infidels to devout Muslims.

After Chris Cuomo came on "New Day," Alisyn

Camerota said, "Trump is using words like jihad and *sharia* as if they were synonyms with extremism." At first, I cringed, but when Cuomo rolled his eyes, I reconsidered my own response. The audience could not see me, but they could see Cuomo, a reporter who is supposed to bring a certain amount of objectivity to his job as well as support for his colleagues.

"Somebody ought to bench Cuomo for letting his feelings show so blatantly," I thought. Granted, Camerota's remarks could have used some editing, but her ignorance might have gone unnoticed to viewers had Cuomo not responded to her remark like a college freshman who wants to beat everyone in the starting lineup to more points.

I used to teach a seminar called, "Journalism and Religion." I believed then, even more so now: Journalists who write and report about religion should learn about the subject matter at hand. If a reporter understands the pillars of Islam, she will know jihad is directly connected to radical Islamic extremism while *sharia* means Islamic law, and in one way or another, effects all Muslims.

Quite frankly, I also wonder sometimes who is advising former Secretary of State Hillary Clinton in her bid for President. While I understand why she would want to stay clear of the word "terrorist," I take issue with Clinton's calling Muslims a "peaceful and tolerant people" who have "nothing whatsoever to do with terrorism." To engage in such a monolithic view of Islam is hardly defensible. Fact is: We are in the midst of a Holy War, exacerbated continuously by cultural clashes and Jihadist attacks.

Jihadists are Muslims, too, more closely akin to Muhammad's pugnacious practices than are the moderate Muslims in America who make a valuable contribution and form a significant voting block. Of course, we want to "keep our people safe," as Clinton said on a campaign stop in New Hampshire, but the multicultural agenda of the early 21st century documented in Professor Diana Eck's ground-breaking *A New Religious America* may need to be re-examined in light of attacks since Sept. 11, 2001. The pluralistic tendency to obscure distinctions inside the religious traditions, particularly Islam, needs to be questioned if we are going to get accurate answers to the 5Ws and an H.

In addition to training journalists, I used to teach courses in multicultural literature. I was passionate about the inclusion of everyone in the so-called "melting pot" of these United States. Once, I even invested in a film being made about the only Japanese regiment to serve on the side of the U.S. in World War II. I still feel passionate about inclusion, but I do not believe we should stretch the facts to protect any one group. We all have to matter if we are going to find our way onto saner ground.

When I tire of watching newscasts and UK Wildcat basketball, I tune into "Person of Interest," "Blindspot," and "Madam Secretary." Or, at least, I used to. I stopped watching "Person of Interest," because it got too violent, and the lead actor no longer reminded me of Jesus in Mel Gibson's equally violent depiction of the crucifixion. In the beginning, "Blindspot" was really interesting, its script a delightful change from lesser portrayals of the iconic gun. Using tattoos on the body of a dark haired woman, with no memory of her past, as clues to her identity struck me as something new, or at least something different from Kardashian fever.

I stopped watching "Blindspot" when it got too violent and turned romantic. I stopped watching "The Good Wife" for a time when Ms. Florrick was on the verge of having an affair with her private investigator as her estranged husband Peter was preparing to run for President. Romantic resolutions are too easy, in life and on film, and I may never forgive Julia Roberts for messing up the filmic adaptation of Elizabeth Gilbert's *Eat, Pray, Love*. If Madam Secretary betrays her professor husband Henry McCord, played by Tim Daly, I will stop watching it, too.

As of the first episode in January, it looks like the McCords are going to make it. The iconic gun, in side profile, took out the evil Russian president, who killed her husband by lethal injection, instead of Madam Secretary.

We may have wondered: Why was it so quiet in the wake of the San Bernardino Massacre after the reporting settled down? Short answer: it wasn't. Militants ambushed unprotected civilians in Turkey, Egypt, Indonesia, and Iraq prior to 28 being killed at the Splendid Hotel in Burkina Faso, West Africa and 22 dead at Bacha Kahn University in Charsadda, Pakistan. Although twice as many people were killed in Burkina Faso as in San Bernardino, the killings received far less coverage. The scant attention paid to attacks outside the United States and Western Europe tends to create a false sense of calm, undergirded by fear.

Is it any accident that two American women, both artistic and blonde, were murdered within one week of each other in different parts of the world? Artist Ashley Olsen was killed in Italy, and TV producer Anne Swaney was killed in Belize. Could these two deaths be another form of Jihad, or is this yet another conspiracy theory, or the real-life model for another TV drama anchored in drugs and sex? Did the killer in Belize, having seen the evening news, "copy cat" the killer in Italy?

These murders happened about two weeks after the New Year's Eve group grope in Cologne, Germany. Some

80 women reportedly were assaulted, and some robbed, by a large group of men who appeared to be organized. Either these men, newly liberated from a strict Islamic regime, thought they could take advantage of "loose" Western women, or what better way to get back at the Infidel than to maul his women? Following the Cologne assault, with similar attacks reported in Hamburg and Stuttgart, the German government, amid protest, looked for ways to deport the Syrian refugees it had welcomed initially.

This chapter has dealt unsparingly with some news reporters who were caught in the drama of the San Bernardino Massacre. I am sympathetic to those who deliver the news, but coverage of the Jihadist attacks should be no exception to keeping cool and reporting with a measure of intelligence on any given day. Reporters don't have to act like Robert Redford or Dustin Hoffman in "All the President's Men" to get better ratings, but a little more investigative reporting coupled with some research on religion couldn't hurt.

As Mary McNamara, Pulitzer Prize-winning television critic for *The Los Angeles Times,* reported shortly after the San Bernardino Massacre: "Just another day in the United States of America, another day of gunfire, panic and fear." McNamara was quoting the BBC's lead to coverage of the mass shootings in southern California.

In his Dec. 3, 2015 "A Word with You" column for the Milwaukee-Wisconsin *Journal Sentinel,* Mark Johnson, also a Pulitzer Prize winner, praised McNamara for driving "straight to the heart of a horrendous news event that many of us watched on television—an all too real reality TV."

On days when newscasts resemble reality TV, I am tempted to speculate that the news died when CBS fired Dan Rather.

CHAPTER VIII

RELIGIOUS INJUNCTIONS AGAINST KILLING

When Moses came down from Mt. Sinai, he carried a tablet of commandments in his arms. Some say they were engraved in stone as instructions from the Lord on how to live less selfishly. The 10 Commandments, as they are called in Judaism and Christianity, form the ethical basis for Krzysztof Kieslowski's "The Decalogue," which means 10. "Thou Shalt Not Kill" is the Sixth Commandment.

When the Buddha started to preach at Sarnath, after his enlightenment under the Bodhi tree at Bodh Gaya, he quickly became aware that his monks and lay followers would need some guidance. He formulated the Five Precepts, the first of which calls for "No Killing," and the Noble Eightfold Path.

The Jains developed a practice known as *ahimsa*, which translates from the Sanskrit as "hurt no living thing." According to Jain Dharma, *ahimsa* is an aid to liberation. Although the practice of non harming was present among Hindus in north India even before Prince Siddhartha became the Buddha, the doctrine of *ahimsa* influenced both Hindu and Buddhist ethics.

Islamic ethics are considerably more complex. While no moderate Muslim would advocate killing, the *Quran* contains 109 verses calling Muslims to war with non-believers for the sake of Islamic rule. These verses are considered to be problematic when Jihadists evoke them as justification for killing. The *Quran* also cautions against starting a fight or killing innocents such as the elderly.

At the far end of the extremist pole in Islam, adherents think there will be a standoff in Jerusalem, and the "armies of Rome" will surrender to Caliphate forces.

The battles may take place with fighters on horseback. From the extreme Jihadist perspective, killing the Infidel is a part of the scenario now unfolding. The Apocalypse is predetermined. Therefore, the killing or beheading of any Heathen is cause for celebration in Jihadist camps. In the movement toward Apocalypse, and the end of the world, Jihadists are hoping to build another "Islamic Golden Age."

The indigenous traditions in North and South America are well known for their respect for the earth and her creatures. For a long time, Indians were portrayed as savages, but multicultural studies reversed the verdict by teaching people about the murder of native peoples by invading Europeans.

Similarly, those who practice witchcraft have been burned at the stake for their vigils. The witches in 17th century New England were thought to be bad women, but there doesn't seem to be much evidence to confirm their wickedness. An electric blue light shot through the bottom of the transparency when the Salem coven of witches, headed by Laurie Cabot, was photographed by *National Geographic* in 1979. Shades of Milarepa.

Injunctions against killing did not prevent Christians from taking up arms. Ask most any non-Christian why he or she does not participate in a Christian community, and the Crusades will quickly come to the forefront of conversation.

Rarely, however, does anyone mention the Crusaders' victims. The Crusaders were out hunting and killing Muslims. Islam must have been a terrible threat to the Popes of Rome, since the Crusades lasted for about two centuries. Both groups wanted control of Jerusalem. In all, eight Crusades were waged from 1096 to 1270.

The religions themselves are not responsible for the

killings, Karen Armstrong would have us believe. Armstrong's view is tantamount to saying: "Not bad religions, just people in need of purification."

Armstrong's view has some merit. As the poet Robert Browning wrote, "we are wonderfully and fearfully made." The religions by themselves may be inadequate, their ethical mandates incapable of corralling a death instinct which has been part of the human psyche since the dawn of time.

Said another way: The desire to kill at lower rungs of the ladder may be stronger than any religious law. As we ascend in consciousness, the murderous instinct can be transmuted. The transmutation has little to do with our specific spiritual or cultural orientation and more to do with the effort we bring to the evolutionary project.

We have reached a point in history at which the religions need to assert their commandments and precepts with greater velocity. Many, especially those which consider themselves to be "modern," have been lax about telling people how to behave for fear they would lose members who do not want to hear any more about "sin" or "hell fire and brimstone." If non-extremist religions fought against killing with the same force Jihadists display in their determination to kill, then the shootings might stop more quickly than anyone could predict.

Assuredly, the killings will not stop so long as the world's religions fail to address the overarching problem of self-hatred. Self-hatred is confined to no one particular religion or culture. Self-hatred is a byproduct of the loss of meaning and purpose, a dilemma which has occupied philosophers since Plato and Aristotle, spilling forward into the work of psychoanalysts such as Sigmund Freud, Carl Jung, and Roberto Assagioli. Brigades of "light workers" are working as well to help us see ourselves more clearly.

The people where I live in south central Kentucky feel strongly about their ethical system based on the 10 Commandments. Many were none too happy when the U.S. Supreme Court found their right to display Moses's laws unconstitutional.

McCreary and Pulaski Counties were ordered to pay $400,000 in legal fees and payments to those who sued. The Supreme Court decided by a vote of 5-4 in favor of the American Civil Liberties Union of Kentucky.

In light of so many killings on U.S. soil since its decision was rendered in 2005, might the Court be inclined to hear the Kentucky case again? It is difficult to say. The decision with regard to the commandments not hanging in the courthouse where Sen. John Sherman Cooper once served as county judge was handed down only four years after the fall of the World Trade Towers in New York. Based on Captain Mark Kelly's figures of 30,000 gun deaths per year, an estimated 300,000 killings have happened in the one decade between 2005 and 2015.

While no thinking person would advocate restriction of freedom in a democracy, neither does it seem rational to assume the number of killings in the United States will decrease automatically by virtue of reasonable argumentation.

Nobody lately has managed to talk a killer out of his gun, and yet, I believe we have to try to lessen the number of guns in the hands of those predisposed to kill. Concomitantly, we could develop more effective ways to address the intense self-hatred which causes humans to murder their own kind.

"It's easier to get a gun in my neighborhood than a computer," said Father Mike Pfleger of Chicago on "Guns in America." Father Pfleger suggested that we title guns in the same way we title cars. The NRA might not like Father Pfleger's idea, but it makes sense, especially coupled with President's Obama's suggestion that "we instill ethical behavior in our kids."

In the religious injunctions against killing, we have much of what we need to stop the brutality. The laws have lain fallow and need to be re-vitalized for purposes of acting as bulwarks to ward off the death instinct. Whether posted in Sen. Cooper's courthouse or not, "Thou Shalt Not Kill" ought to be engraved in every thinking person's heart. Coupled with therapy, and help from former killers who have transformed, "No Killing" could become an effective teaching once more.

If we believe in the efficacy of grace, now is the time to ask for a transfusion. If we identify as agnostic or atheist, we can transform the structures of reality by the ways in which we work with our minds. Clear thinking and feeling go a long way toward the process of evolution.

As the youngest of the world's religions, with a contingent predisposed to killing, Islam could enhance its teachings by borrowing some maturity from its elders. Islam is, after all, the youngest of the world's religions, and sometimes its youth shows. Especially in areas where Islam is friendly to other religions, moderate Muslims are far less rambunctious than their fundamentalist brothers and sisters. Among radical sects, a concession to *ahimsa* is unlikely. As the late Ayatollah Khomeini said, "It is a great joy to kill and be killed for Allah."

CHAPTER IX

WHAT THE MASS GRAVES MEAN

From 1915-1917, an estimated 800,000 to 1.5 million were killed in the Ottoman government's systematic extermination of the Armenian minority inside its homeland.

From 1941-1945, some six million Jews and five million non-Jewish victims were killed by Adolf Hitler's Nazi regime and its collaborators.

During the nine-month long war for independence in 1971, members of the Pakistani military and supporting militias killed an estimated 300,000 to 3,000,000 in East Pakistan, or what is now Bangladesh.

Between 1975 and 1979, the Khmer Rouge killed approximately two million people in the "killing fields" of Cambodia.

During 1992-1995, 8,000 Muslims and another 25,000 to 30,000 civilians were killed by Serbs in an ethnic cleansing campaign in the Bosnian war.

In his online article entitled "The Worst Genocides of the 20th and 21st Centuries," Piero Scaruffi lists victims of additional genocides totaling 32,295,000. Added to the victims listed above, Scaruffi's figure gives us a total of 52,833,500 people who have been killed in the 20th and early 21st centuries by tyrants, 800,000 of these people in Rwanda.

It's a staggering figure: 52,833,500 people were *genocided* in one century alone from 1915-2015. Spelled out, that's almost fifty-three million people murdered.

Actually, the figure may be low. Scaruffi includes a question mark instead of numbers for the Chinese occupation of Tibet. While the Chinese seem to think the tiny nation high in the Himalayas belongs to them, and it is their right to turn a peace-loving place into another Las Vegas, His Holiness the Dalai Lama has traveled the world over encouraging support for the campaign to "Free Tibet."

According to a Radio Lhasa broadcast of Oct. 1, 1960, 87,000 Tibetans were killed in the 1959 Uprising, but Tibetan exiles cite the figure dead at 430,000 with more Tibetans killed in subsequent years. Other sources estimate Tibetans killed by the Chinese to be around 1.2 million.

If the later number is accurate, that would bring the number of people killed by tyrants from 1915-2015 to 54,033,500. Spelled out, that's fifty-four million, thirty-three thousand, and five-hundred.

According to a July 20, 1999 *Chicago Tribune* article headed "What about Human Rights in Tibet?" by Daniel John Sobieski, "Communist China's aim remains the total and systematic elimination of Tibetan religion and culture."

Between 1959 and 1961, most of Tibet's 6,259 monasteries were destroyed. In 1976, the eight remaining monasteries were forced to teach Marxism. Tour guides who take Westerners around parts of Tibet have been known to say the monasteries were destroyed by "natural disasters."

Tibet is one of the most alarming examples of ethnic cleansing in modern times. By no means, however, does Tibet stand alone. Virtually all the mass killings cited here are examples of attempts to rid the planet of people whose cultural, racial, or religious makeup is different from the majority.

In the West, the Holocaust, understandably, looms large over other ethnic cleansings. In terms of the sheer volume of people exterminated—statistics vary from 11 to 12 million—the Holocaust wiped more beings off the earth than the Armenian, Bangladeshi, Bosnian, Cambodian, and Tibetan genocides combined.

"Son of Saul," a 2015 addition to Holocaust cinema, won the Grand Prix at the Cannes Film Festival. The debut film of Hungarian director Laszlo Nemes, "Son of Saul" examines life inside the camps from the perspective of a *Sonderkommando*, or one who was responsible for herding people to the gas chambers. "Son of Saul" may help us to learn more about genocide from the point of view of both perpetrator and victim.

"Never again!" was the shot heard around the world at the end of World War II in response to the atrocities in Nazi Germany. Bombs do not count? The United States dropped two big ones on Hiroshima and Nagasaki, killing an estimated 246,000 and leaving large numbers to die from radiation sickness. The number of Japanese dead are not included in Scaruffi's List, perhaps because President Harry S. Truman used nuclear power to persuade the Japanese to surrender. When the bombs were dropped, the United States and Japan were still officially at war. Official wartime statistics do not always count as genocide.

The ethics surrounding American use of nuclear power in Japan are still debated. Some insist the Japanese would never have come to their knees, since they were first to bomb Pearl harbor—there was honor to defend—while others claim the bombings of Hiroshima and Nagasaki were an unnecessary display of power to get back at the Japanese. Indeed, it behooves us to ask if any of the mass graves resulting from democratic motives or power grabs have accomplished anything other than perpetuation of inhumane patterns

The term "genocide" was coined by Raphael Lemkin in 1944, a likely year for such a coinage to appear.

"Genocide" is defined in Article 2 of The Convention on the Prevention and Punishment of the Crime of Genocide (CPPCG) of 1948 as "deliberately" calculating to kill or cause serious harm to a national, ethical, racial, or religious group.

In other words, one group gets together and decides it does not want to associate with another group it deems to be different from, and usually inferior to, itself. Then, group #1 elects to exterminate group #2, and in some cases, if group #2 has survivors, keep it from reproducing more of itself as in China's attempt to obliterate Tibetan blood by inter-marrying Tibetans to Han Chinese.

In terms of the definition offered by CPPCG, we could say the Jihadists of radical Islam have committed genocide against the United States of America. Over 3,000 have been exterminated on American soil in the name of eradicating the Infidel from planet earth. Newscasters do not typically refer to Jihadist killings as genocide, as the U.S. is a super power, and super powers are thought by some to be tyrants. But, Osama bin Laden is on Scaruffi's List with 3,500 dead beside his name. Three-thousand and five-hundred when compared with 54,033,500 is a drop in the proverbial bucket of the worst genocides committed, but the fall of the World Trade Towers affected hundreds of family members as well.

The United States was the aggressor in Vietnam, an unpopular war among my generation. The shootings at Kent State on May 4, 1970 were deeply troubling. The Ohio National Guard *fired 67 rounds over a period of 13 seconds* (italics mine), killing four unarmed students and wounding nine others, one of whom suffered permanent paralysis. After the fact, the Kent State shootings were referred to as the "Kent State Massacre."

The students were gathered to protest the Cambodian Campaign which President Richard Nixon announced during a television address on April 30. Nixon is on Scaruffi's List as having disposed of 70,000 Vietnamese and Cambodian civilians from 1969-1974. President Lyndon Johnson is listed, too, with 30,000 deaths in Vietnam from 1963-1968 beside his name. These are wartime deaths. Nonetheless, Scaruffi lists them as genocide.

For his coverage of the war in Cambodia, Sydney Schanberg won the 1976 Pulitzer Prize for International Reporting. He wrote about the Pakistani genocide in what is now Bangladesh before being transferred to southeast Asia to cover the war in Vietnam for *The New York Times*.

After the Americans left, Schanberg chose to stay in Phnom Penh during the Communist takeover. His friendship and professional affiliation with Cambodian photojournalist Dith Pran is documented in his book, *The Death and Life of Dith Pran*, on which the film, "The Killing Fields," is based.

As an American, Schanberg could leave southeast Asia, but Dith Pran could not. He was trapped in Cambodia during "year zero" when Pot Pol and the Khmer Rouge killed about two million people. For a long period of time, Dith Pran nearly starved in a labor camp, but he finally managed to escape.

Dith Pran's journey across a 40-mile stretch of skeletons and skulls, which he named "the killing fields," appears as an unforgettable part of the film. His escape enters the realm of the mythic. Barefoot and alone, he confronts the face of death at virtually every turn. His traverse is one of the most effective presentations of the journey motif on record.

Eventually, Dith Pran was reunited with Sydney Schanberg, made his way to the United States, and worked as a photojournalist for *The New York Times*. He became an American citizen and lived in New Jersey.

I got to meet Dith Pran when he visited Allegheny College. Students were strongly encouraged to attend his talk. Afterwards, I told Dith Pran how much his story had meant to me and how much I appreciated his courage. He smiled quietly, modestly.

Dith Pran died in 2008 at age 65. He died young. No wonder. His escape from the Khmer Rouge was no walk in the park.

Would I, if I had that moment to re-live with Dith Pran, tell him the whole truth of my response to "The Killing Fields?"

The deeper texture, the subtext, is this: When Dith Pran and Sydney Schanberg were reunited in the film, and John Lennon's "Imagine" came up on the sound track, I began to cry; I couldn't stop crying; I cried to the point of bawling; I was crying out of happiness for Sydney Schanberg and Dith Pran; I was crying, because friendship between men is so seldom represented warmly in cinema; I was crying for two million Cambodians who are no longer here to cry with me; I was crying for eleven million who were gassed in the camps in Germany, six million of them Jews; I was crying for Pot Pol, too, and for all the tyrants who have been so callous as to think that ridding the planet of any human flesh could ever be an argument for keeping the population explosion in check, or an answer to humanity's woes.

"Pray for the Chinese," the Dalai Lama said when asked about Tibet's oppressors, "pray for the Chinese."

More than likely, if I had my moment to live over

with Dith Pran, I would let it stand in its stillness. When I recall that encounter now, I think of Carolyn Forche's advice to activists and journalists assigned to political beats.

Now Director of the Lannan Center for Poetics and Social Practice, Forche holds the Lannan Chair in Poetry at Georgetown University. Her reputation was secured by a number of poems exploring the brutality she personally experienced in El Salvador, poems which appear in *The Country Between Us*, her second collection.

Forche's advice to aspiring activists and journalists still rings in my head as I write *A Short Book about Killing:* "Be cool."

"Cool" is the word to describe John Lennon's performance video of "Imagine" on YouTube. In the video, John and Yoko are walking toward a white house with Athenian pillars and busts of patriarchs on the front porch. They open the door and enter. John seats himself at a white baby grand, and Yoko opens the shutters of the long windows, so the light can come into the large and largely empty room. John is dressed in a black suit, Yoko in a white floor length gown.

John begins to sing the lyrics to "Imagine," and Yoko seats herself beside him at the piano. They look at each other. Then, they look toward the camera.

John and Yoko's video of "Imagine" is a perfect representation of life in a state in which the drive for power and the need to kill are obliterated.

No action. No conflict. No pull from the past or tension in the present. No boundaries to defend.

Imagine such a world where we wouldn't have to ask what the mass graves mean. Imagine a world without them. Imagine what could happen if each of us turned the drive to purify inward. Imagine if the number 54,035,500 were reduced to zero in a future century.

If we don't try, we will have no choice but to reproduce "the killing fields" as if they never existed before.

CHAPTER X

JEFF'S SONG: A PARADIGM FOR NON HARMING

Think mainly of life. Life proceeds from the inside out. When you think of death, do so consciously. Mindfully.

Lay all the guns and weapons of mass destruction at the feet of Shiva, Buddha, Christ, Allah—or human reason.

Respect the earth and her bounty, trees and cows included. Pray especially for the polar bear's plight.

Forgive everyone on your list of enemies, especially children, ex-spouses or partners, and friends who have betrayed you. As Richard Hugo once wrote: "Love everyone you can. The list gets longer and shorter."

Stop "othering" human beings as well as nations and cultures.

Do not watch any movie or TV show, or play any video game which features killing. Boycott violence.

Rest more and work less. No need to test your strength or your ability to tolerate alcohol, nicotine, opiates, or sugar.

Spend at least one hour per day doing nothing. Just be still.

If you fail to move toward a paradigm for non harming, consider your disappointment an opening, and keep trying.

A number of years ago, I read an article in *Ms.* magazine entitled "Ruth's Song" by Gloria Steinem. I was deeply affected by Steinem's article about her mother, and I used her piece several times in my journalism class as an example of good magazine writing, writing to be emulated. Writers often complain about their parents, but Steinem found ways to celebrate her mother's life without resorting to harsh criticism or overly wrought emotion.

I also selected passages from Martin Luther King, Jr.'s "Letter from a Birmingham Jail" and asked aspiring

journalists to model his passion as well as his tone. Toward
the end of "Letter from a Birmingham Jail," King uses
repetition of when clauses to reinforce his call for justice in
modulations as appropriate to Alabama in 1968 as they
would have been for the 2015 Memorial Service at Emanuel
African Methodist Episcopal Church in Charleston when
President Barack Obama sang "Amazing Grace."

    I hadn't yet encountered Bro. Wayne Teasdale's
work when the World Trade Towers fell, but I had just
shifted from training journalists to teaching comparative
religions in the Fall semester of 2001, one of two terms I
taught at Somerset Community College. Although I
recognize the value of community colleges, and actually got
a good start myself at SCC, I wasn't a very effective teacher
in this venue. I had spent nearly 20 years sitting in a circle
with students in the snow belt talking about the meaning of
the meaning, and when I returned to Kentucky to help my
parents as they aged, I figured teaching a course or two
would be a good idea. Teaching to the test was not one of
my strengths. I wound up at UK in the Honors Program
back in the company of the circular dialogue, the very
determined, and the very adverse to Bs.

    One morning, some 14 years after I stood watching
the first Trade Tower crumble on a TV screen at SCC, I was
reviewing a section of Wayne Teasdale's book *The Mystic
Heart* for a retreat to be held at Slate Branch Ashram in
conjunction with The Community of The Mystic Heart on
"The Nine Elements of Mature Interspirituality." A name
in Teasdale's chapter on "Deep Nonviolence" nearly caused
me to leap from my chair and into the woods.

    Jeff Genung.

    I knew Jeff was a friend of Wayne Teasdale's, as I
had previously read the story Wayne included in *The Mystic*

Heart about Jeff's encounter with a doe in upstate New York. Having had a fair number of transformative experiences myself in that neck of the woods, I once wrote about a deer who got on my path and inspired a *villanelle* entitled, "The Mother's Woods," a place "where deer roam free."

Living in Kentucky now, I am intensely aware of the role guns have played in rural culture. Hunting is popular. At Slate Branch Farm, we post a "No Trespassing" sign, and when I hear the sound of guns in the distance, I whisper, "Run, babies, run. Come here. You will be safe over by the cave where Cherokees once lived."

In his late teens, Jeff liked to go deer hunting alone. One day, he shot a doe but failed to kill her outright. As he stood in front of the dying animal, he saw "infinite gentleness" in her eyes. There was "no fear or hostility." To use Wayne Teasdale's words, she seemed to be saying: "Don't worry. It's okay. I forgive you and love you."

The doe who would not die is somewhat like the taxi driver in Krzysztof Kieslowski's "A Short Film about Killing." Neither the doe nor the man died rapidly. Whereas Jacek expressed no remorse when his victim kept gasping for breath, the main character in Teasdale's story was touched to the quick.

During his years of hunting, Jeff had never come this close to his prey. Overcome with grief, he made a commitment to non harming. The doe was Jeff's teacher. According to *The Mystic Heart*, she gave him "an indelible lesson in the mystery of life and the interconnectedness of all beings."

I meditated for a bit to get my bearings. Then, I began to type an email to Jeff Genung. We had been working on an Interspiritual project together with Kurt

Johnson and Yanni Maniates and had made plans to speak on the telephone after the Christmas holidays. That Jeff was the man in Teasdale's text who took the doe's spirit into himself and changed his life hadn't registered during our previous email exchanges. Sometimes, beauty can be closer than the breath, and we cannot see it.

"Change your life," said the poet Ranier Maria Rilke, author of *Letters to a Young Poet*. Were it that we human beings of all ages could take the poet's advice to heart and learn to sing "Jeff's Song" as beautifully as he sings it himself.

I could steer clear of emotion and begin to end this book with a flat-footed chapter called, "Alternatives to Killing." I could list a number of practical tasks we could undertake to lessen the number of people we lose every day in a country where 88 to 92 people are killed by guns. Fact is, however, both thought and feeling are important in the evolutionary project.

I will list just one: Practical Task #1: If it isn't too obvious, we could give up our guns without a fight at the OK Corral or on Capitol Hill. If we don't have any guns, we won't be tempted to fire them.

Here we are in Kieslowski's apartment building, however, and we are waiting to see how the story ends: There's Maestro Moses, a Jew from the Middle East who plays his music upstairs; Prince Siddhartha, a north Indian ex-patriot who gave up his castle for freedom; Jain Dhamawoski, who has no hair—had it all pulled out for a cameo appearance as a monk; Hesus Hernandez, a Latino activist who throws chairs; Muhammad Malikini whose got a stash of A-15s parked in his closet: there's a guy from Colorado who died his hair; a guy from South Carolina who won't take down his rebel flag; there's Mitch and Macey

Maloney who claim they have made millions starring in a grade B movie. Going up and down, up and down, in the elevator of Kieslowski's Universal Estate, much like the rungs of *The Divine Comedy*, others appear who prefer to remain anonymous. They rarely speak in the shaft, but their lives overlap by virtue of the species they inhabit.

It isn't looking real good for the cast at this late date in human history—in *Kali Yuga*, a very dark time period. They are trapped in a movie of their own making. They are worn out from too many gigs, too many affairs, too many battles, too many guns, knives, and hatchets. But, as Dante told Homer, with Vyasa and Willie listening in, "I am *insufferably* optimistic about the fate of this bunch and their ability to pull it out."

I am, too. And, actually, although this is not reality TV, that bit about being *insufferably optimistic* is mine. I spoke that line to Kurt Johnson over pasta at a neighborhood restaurant in lower Manhattan. I am a model for Eudora Welty's *The Optimist's Daughter,* but I gave the line to Dante here, because he has more clout than I do as a simple monk. I fuss at Kurt for working too hard, but I not so secretly admire his tireless efforts as a sacred activist, and my inscribed copy of *The Coming Interspiritual Age* is lined with notes. Kurt had a lot to do with the last point in the paradigm for non harming featured prominently to open this chapter. He regards everything as an opening which can get as exhausting as the interminable conversation in "My Dinner with Andre," a film I like almost as much as Krzysztof Kieslowski's "Decalogue." When there's work to do, Kurt and I agree, we have to pick ourselves up, uplift each other as best we can, and keep on trucking.

When I think about the dear ones I refer to as "compatriots," I remember another special Allegheny moment with the poet Denise Levertov. We were friends until late in her good life, and even though she didn't feel much like traveling from Boston, she came out to northwestern Pennsylvania to accept an honorary doctorate. President Dan Sullivan wanted me to come back in off sabbatic to award Levertov's degree, *honoris causa,* and I obliged. Levertov had visited Allegheny previously, and I had visited her home out near Tufts where she taught before moving to Seattle. I wanted to honor a relationship dating back to my senior year at Union when Dr. Frank Merchant, in his tweed jacket and bow tie, inscribed some lines from William Carlos Williams into our young minds for all time: "It is difficult to get the news from poems yet we die miserably every day for lack of what is found there."

At her reading in Ford Chapel, we were waiting for the crowd to filter in—no one confiscated back packs to search for guns in the 1990s—and I wanted to check a line with Levertov to include in my introduction of her to the Allegheny community. I had first heard her read from "Life at War" my senior year at Union, 46 years prior to the murder of Prof. Sarah Hendrix. In those days, Levertov traveled around the country urging everyone to oppose the war in Vietnam.

I leaned in toward Levertov's curly head and spoke the last line of her poem which I consider to be as representative of a certain historical period in American poetry as is Adrienne Rich's "Transcendental Etude"—and as good.

"Would," Levertov corrected me gently. Nothing has the "deep intelligence" living at peace *would* have.

We live in the conditional tense most of our lives, and when we find our way to moments of steadfastness, we touch down deep into what the Indians call *iccha shakti,* the energy of will. A Westerner with an Eastern bent, the German philosopher Arthur Schopenhauer, a precursor to Freud with Buddhist inclinations, knew about this kind of will. He wrote a book called *The World as Will*, or *The World as My Idea*, which I encountered initially in a seminar at Emory with an unforgettable professor named Bobby Paul who later forged the Emory-Tibet Partnership. The world can be no different from how we see it, Schopenhauer maintained, and how we think it into existence. The world takes shape from the inside out as does life in its multiplicity.

Of course, if we are theologically inclined, as am I, we co-create the world with our Higher Power. We may call HP God, Shiva, Buddha, Christ, Allah, or the Holy Spirit as he is known by a number of names across spiritual traditions.

In my view, HP dwells at the center of the universe as well as inside each of us. HP lives inside us in a tiny lotus we can access by getting still, closing our eyes, and focusing on the breath. Sometimes, HP appears as a scintillating blue pearl.

In my humble opinion, we are chips off the old block. When Brahma, or God, created us, she left a part of herself in our minds, hearts, and bodies. And, when we discover Her or Him as our very own Self, there is no more need to violate the precious commandments handed down through Interspiritual apostles across time.

We are basically good. It's just that many of us don't know it. When we are trapped in self-defeating patterns rooted in "me, me, me," it may feel as if we are "Waiting for Godot" or an Arabian Knight to come fix us.

Divinity is not something altogether apart from who we are. Said another way, Brahma lives inside us as *Atma-*

Svarupa or the Self. When we lose touch with our own Divinity, or separate ourselves from it, we can easily mess up and do things we might not do otherwise. Ethics tend to take a back seat when we are focused solely on what our egos want and how to get it.

As my Guru said several years ago during a morning program at her ashram in upstate New York, it is not the four-legged creature who concerns me. It is the two-legged creature.

Usually, my Guru speaks in glowing terms about humanity and our capacity for greatness. On this particular day, she was speaking about nature, as I recall, and encouraging us to take better care of the planet. Her insight is instructive here as well. She has written elsewhere about discarding the weight of self-hatred.

Our disregard for the earth is part of the same paradigm that leads to death and destruction. It is a worldview that values power over goodness, prestige over simplicity, fame over honest self-assessment and regard. There is nothing wrong with worldly success—in fact, pleasure and prosperity are included in the Four Goals of Life for Hindus—but something is terribly askew if we allow the drives for pleasure and power to overtake us.

When we two-legged creatures try to hide from our basic goodness by covering it over with our own selfish wants, or denying it, we can easily get stuck in our own sense of self-importance. In such ego-driven states, we are capable of making great mischief and doing great harm. If we can take what Joanna Macey, a Buddhist, calls the "Tantric flip," and learn to see with writers like Flannery O'Connor, a Roman Catholic, that even evil can be part of a movement toward the greater good, then we can co-create with our Higher Power an astonishing world in which there is no more killing, and goodness prevails.

The problem of killing, as I see it, begins on the inside and manifests in material reality in direct approximation to our internal makeup. If we are murky and messed up inside, we project a virtual swamp onto others. If we have done some work to clean up the marsh, then our projections are far less dangerous to others and to ourselves.

If I am convinced of anything about killing, about the various kinds of killings we continue to witness in our times, it is this: Killing is an expression of self-hatred. Teach our children to think well of themselves, and to "know a little something about *bodhicitta,*" as I heard Dr. Vincent Dummer say in another context at the Shambhala Buddhist Center of Lexington, and they most likely will not grow up needing to take their ugly feelings out on others and themselves. They will know how to let the energy of basic goodness inform and direct their lives.

Case in point: A photograph of Christopher Harper-Mercer, Roseburg, Oregon, all dressed up in his suit with nowhere to go. Like any number of ISIS killers, he had never held a girl's hand, and the prospect of dying famous was more attractive to him than continuing to live as a jerk, all caught up in feelings of resentment and sexual frustration.

Further case in point: Syed Farook, angry and humorless, with a new baby girl he raised in the midst of pipe bombs and rounds of ammunition. Even his child was a "prop," TV commentators said following the San Bernardino Massacre, and after all was said and done—wife dead, hard drive disposed of, friend hauled in for being an accomplice—Farook was stripped of his humanity just as he sought to rob others of theirs.

As simple minded as it seems, it would be far better for everyone concerned to just go by the First Buddhist Precept, "No Killing," the Sixth Commandment, "Thou Shalt Not Kill," or the Hindu-Jain idea of *ahimsa*, "hurt no living thing," and be done with it. Regarding other human beings as Infidels, and taking the liberty to remove them from the planet, is a serious example of "othering" which needs to be examined carefully by those who subscribe to the practice. If we are all to share the planet, murdering others is not theologically, philosophically, or ethically justifiable.

In the 1970s, Adrienne Rich's "Transcendental Etude" was published in a celebrated collection of poems entitled *The Dream of a Common Language* (1977). Rich's poem opens with the image of a doe, all four fawns springing after her "into the dark maples."

I felt the first stanza of Rich's poem acutely when I read Wayne Teasdale's account of Jeff Genung and the deer who looked directly into his eyes after he had shot her. It is clear that Jeff would not shoot the doe if he encountered her again. I would bet there are others out there, too, who are feeling drawn toward a paradigm of non harming.

Spike Lee certainly is. On Dec. 1, 2015, he lead a march against gun violence down Broadway to Times Square after his most recent film, "Chi-Raq," premiered in New York City. Then, he brokered a partnership between the National Basketball Association and Everytown for Gun Safety, founded by former mayor Michael Bloomberg, for a series of public service announcements opposing gun violence to air on Christmas day.

Michael Beard certainly was when he founded the National Coalition to Ban Handguns in 1974. Now with 48 affiliates, the organization changed its name to the Coalition to Stop Gun Violence in 1989. Joshua Horowitz, its executive director, blogs regularly on gun violence. As Moms Demand Action for Gun Sense in America is well aware, "hurt no living thing" is more than just a nice thought. It is a teaching to hold in the forefront of our minds and to live by moment by moment. Mahatma Gandhi used the teaching consciously to thwart the British Raj, with its fondness for military pomposity, and ultimately chase all those in khaki pants bearing arms back to their own island. Martin Luther King, Jr. learned the workings of *ahimsa* from Gandhi. His tributary of the Civil Rights Movement was anchored in this Sanskrit word, sometimes translated as compassion.

President Barack Obama is trying to move the United States toward a paradigm of non harming by introducing sensible restrictions and declaring he will not vote or campaign for anyone who does not support gun reform. If we are concerned about what we may consider to be Obama's covert attempts to take our guns away, then why don't we just give them to him? He might be able to recycle some of the parts to help pay down the national debt.

In his book entitled *The Splendor of Recognition*, Sw. Shantananda tells the story of a monk in an expanded state of consciousness who was traveling on an Indian train. A man approached the monk with a pistol and thrust it in his face. The monk was experiencing such unconditional love in the moment that he did not perceive the intruder as a potential killer. "Nice gun," the monk said, and the man dropped the threat at once.

Granted, most of us do not live in an exalted state most of the time, but the story of the monk and the man with a gun poses an alternative to the fear many people experience when threatened. As shown in rape cases, fear entices would-be attackers. Strength, confidence, and good will tend to send negative intentions fleeing.

"The Doctor" and his group of Vigilantes are working to disrupt and cripple the spread of Jihadist propaganda online. Vigilante Potato Head says he is "too busy being part of a civilized and functioning society" to join ISIS. There's hope here. As the late APJ Kalam, former President of India and a Muslim, told me in a private conversation at the University of Kentucky not long before I took a group of Honors Program students to visit with him at his residence in New Delhi: "The next world war is likely to be fought in cyberspace."

A number of organizations exist which oppose radical Islam and Jihadists. Some appear to be legitimate, while others seem to be in the business of projecting pre-existing fear and anger onto a particular issue. It is best to investigate and have a personal experience of such groups before joining or sending donations online.

Just as Robert De Niro wore a green ribbon in solidarity with the murdered children of Atlanta, we all could join Moms Demand Action's "orange walks." We could put on MDA's orange caps and walk in the name of keeping our children free from harm. We could post messages on Social Media discouraging violence. If digital activism is our thing, we could join the Hactivists Network Anonymous, but it's wise to be careful here: Too much mocking borders on "othering" and can have an adverse effect. We could support President Obama 's initiatives instead of engaging in yet another conspiracy theory rooted in fear.

Ultimately, killing is a problem that belongs to us all—in real life and in the movies. Killing could not manifest if it did not first exist in consciousness. Spike Lee joins Krzysztof Kieslowski and a handful of filmmakers who have addressed the issue mindfully, and with a sense of history, his "Chi-Raq" based on the Greek drama, the "Lysistrata." In Lee's re-telling, a group of determined women in Chicago bands together and demands that their husbands and lovers put down their weapons, or lose their intimate privileges.

Perhaps other filmmakers will follow Spike Lee's lead and lay down their focus on destruction. On Christmas day 2015, the number of advertisements for upcoming TV programs, movies, and video games featuring the iconic gun in juxtaposition with the PSAs against gun violence was shocking.

Taking a station break now to issue a message to anyone who is thinking of killing, or planning to kill: Please be prepared to witness your prey up close, to feel his warm breath, to see the sadness in his eyes, to know beyond doubt that you will break the hearts of his loved ones if you kill.

As the poet Wanda Fries who teaches at SCC posted on Social Media in the wake of San Bernardino: Killing used to be "so personal."

If you commit murder, or genocide, please have the decency to plead guilty and accept the consequences. There is nothing more cowardly than a killer who tries to save himself at his victim's expense, and yet, this killer, too, as a member of the human race, stands to benefit from the compassion we all can muster, however weakly or strongly felt.

Unlike Jacek in "A Short Film about Killing," if you kill, please be grateful for the last gift you are offered on earth, even if it falls short of being an unfiltered cigarette or a reward in heaven.

In the final analysis, there is more wisdom in tenderness than in leaving the doe to die in her own blood.

CHAPTER XI

LETTER TO A JIHADIST FROM A HEATHEN

Dear Jihadist,

As I write these words, I am wondering if you are watching television coverage of the San Bernardino Massacre. I suspect you are. I suspect you find parts of it to be funny. And parts make you feel powerful. After all, you now have conducted three major attacks on the United States of America: Flying into the World Trade Towers, setting off bombs at the Boston Marathon, spraying bodies with bullets at a holiday gathering in southern California.

I don't know if your name is ISIS, al-Qaeda, Hamas, or some other moniker which spells terror. The intent of your work is the same. You want to hurt and maim the Heathen in the name of Allah. I would be ashamed. The God this Heathen knows isn't impressed with murder and mayhem and would prefer not to deal with an Apocalypse any time soon.

And yet, I also suspect that you have been wounded very deeply. When American planes bombed your land, you felt afraid and bewildered. You felt *occupied,* body and nation. You wanted to hit back at the giant Infidel who threatened to swallow your culture. You did not want to be westernized, and that is your right.

And so, you did strike back. Down came the symbols of wealth and power. Off came the limbs of runners in a city at the heart of American freedom. Across the room, bullets flew as 14 gave their lives at Christmas, their deaths a wreath sparkling in the distance.

Dear Jihadist, these were real people. Warm blood flowed through their veins. They had families who mourn.

Did they deserve to die uselessly? Their blood was no less sacred than yours.

Frequently, I have entertained fantasies of traveling around the country, from the craggy coasts of Maine to the wetlands of Washington, and inviting people to surrender their guns at the feet of this God you call Allah. As a Heathen, I do not worship Allah, as you well know, even though I believe there is essentially no difference between your God and mine. Or, the magnificent force which some decline to identify as divine.

If I conducted a gun-surrendering tour, would you shoot me? It might depend on how much television coverage my death would attract. Or, how much mileage you could get from my blood on Facebook.

In the wake of the San Bernardino Massacre, I expect you will strike again, but not until this hit has settled down. To keep the Heathen afraid and off balance—that appears to be your ammunition.

Soon, there could be backlash against moderate Muslims in the United States, people who place little stock in Muhammad's warlord tactics. These Muslims say they want nothing to do with you, and yet, you both address your God as Allah. In some ways, you are closer to the Prophet with your surprise attacks, his invention. Your modern Western counterparts may have to shout, or love you down, to get you to quit spitting bullets. Then again, what success do relatives usually have when they try to silence angry adolescents?

Dear Jihadist, I could call you a coward, a lost and lonely child. I could whisper in your ear for only you to hear: Mature men and women step into the light, state their grievances, and declare war in honorable fashion.

However, I no more believe that there is such an

entity as a monolithic Jihadist than I would ask you to accept me or my brothers and sisters as Infidels all of one stripe. Nor, do I find aggression against you to be acceptable. We have come to a point in time, it seems, when war is unthinkable. The earth can stand no more of our antics.

I fear for you, dear Jihadist, and no less for me and my kind. We must all learn to smile at fear. Otherwise, we are stuck in a desert of our own making, a desolate place where sand swirls wild, and "othering" blinds us to what we do not understand.

Maybe we both suffer from ideological blindspots? Maybe we end up mirroring each other while acting in each other's dramas? Perhaps we could stop the killings long enough to clean the mirror, examine our fear, and learn how to forgive.

With love,
Sw. Shraddhananda
The Heathen

P.S.: *Smile at Fear* is the title of a book by Chogyam Trungpa Rinpoche, a Tibetan spiritual leader who fled his country on foot in 1959 with the Chinese chasing his small entourage across the Himalayas.

Bibliography

Dante Alighieri. *The Divine Comedy.* John Ciardi, tr. Norton, 1977.

Aristophanes. *Lysistrata.* Jeffrey Henderson, tr. Focus, 1988.

Karen Armstrong. *Fields of Blood.* Anchor Books, 2015.

Hal Ashby. "Coming Home." Jerome Hellman Productions, Jayne Productions, Inc. 1978.

Charles Baudelaire. *Selected Poems.* Carol Clark, ed. Penguin, 1996.

Michael Bay. "13 Hours: The Secret Soldiers of Benghazi." Arts Entertainment, Dune Films, Latina Pictures, 2016.

Samuel Beckett. "Waiting for Godot." Grove Press, 2011.

Peter Berger. *Holy War, Inc.: Inside the Secret World of Osama bin Laden.* Free Press, 2002.

Carl Bernstein and Bob Woodward. *All the President's Men.* Simon and Schuster, 1974.

William Victor Blacoe. *From Saul to Paul: The Road to Apostleship.* Cedar Fort, 2014.

Rice Broocks. *God's Not Dead: Evidence for God in an Age of Uncertainty.* Thomas Nelson, 2015.

Michael A. Brown and Daniel M. Gerstein. "Anonymous vs. ISIS: Wishing the vigilante hackers luck against the murderous jihadists." *New York Daily News,* Dec. 14, 2015.

Robert Browning. *The Norton Critical Edition.* James F. Loucks and Andrew M. Stauffer, eds. Norton, 2007.

Vincent Bugliosi. *Helter Skelter.* Norton, 2001.

John Calipari. "UK Wildcat Men's Basketball." CBS, ESPN, SEC Network, 2009-present.

Albert Camus. *The Stranger.* Vintage, 1989.

Truman Capote. *In Cold Blood.* Vintage, 1994.

Sw. Chidvilasananda. *Enthusiasm.* SYDA, 1997.

Malcolm Clark. *Islam for Dummies.* For Dummies, 2011.

Anderson Cooper and President Barack Obama. "Guns in America." CNN, Jan. 7, 2015.

Simon Cottee. "Why It's So Hard to Stop ISIS Propaganda." *The Atlantic,* March 2, 2015.

John Donne. *Collected Poetry.* Christopher Ricks, ed. Penguin, 2012.

Jamie Doward. "Media Coverage of Terrorist 'Leads to Further Violence.'" *The Guardian,* Aug. 1, 2015.

Marianne Dresser, ed. *Buddhist Women on the Edge: Contemporary Perspectives from the Western Frontier.* North Atlantic Books, 1996.

Colin Dwyer. "Donald Trump: 'I could shoot somebody, and I wouldn't lose any voters.'" NPR, Jan. 23, 2016.

Clint Eastwood. "American Sniper." Warner Brothers, 2014.

Diana Eck. *A New Religious America.* HarperSanFrancisco, 2002.

"El Chapo Escape Video." CNN, Jan. 11, 2016.

T. S. Eliot. *The Waste Land, Prufrock and Other Poems.* Neeland Media LLC, 2009.

Oriana Fallaci. *Letter to a Child Never Born.* Anchor Press, 1978.

Abolqasem Ferdowsi. *Shanameh: The Epic of the Persian Kings.* Dick Davis, tr. Viking, 2006.

Sally Fitzgerald, ed. *The Habit of Being: Letters of Flannery O'Connor.* Farrar, Straus and Giroux, 1979.

Carolyn Forche, ed. *Against Forgetting: Twentieth Century Poetry of Witness.* Norton, 1993.

Carolyn Forche. *The Country Between Us.* Copper Canyon Press, 1981.

Sigmund Freud. *Civilization and its Discontents.* James Strachey, tr. Norton, 2010.

_____. *The Freud Reader.* Peter Gay, ed. Norton, 1995.

Claire Galofarro. "Ky. triple homicide shocks victims' social worker friends." The Louisville *Courier Journal,* Feb. 21, 2015. Re-printed in *USA Today,* Feb. 22, 2015.

Jeff Genung. "Contemplative Life." contemplative life.org

Soumik Ghosh. "Blindspot." NBC, 2015-present.

Mel Gibson. "The Passion of the Christ." Screenplay, Mel Gibson, Benedict Fitzgerald, and William Fulco. Icon Productions, 2004.

Elizabeth Gilbert. *Eat, Pray, Love.* Riverhead Books, 2007.

William Giraldi. "Swimming Upstream: The Frustrations, Enlightening, Dizzying Career of Stanley Fish." *New Republic,* Oct. 12, 2015.

Rene Girard. *Violence and the Sacred.* Patrick Gregory, tr. Johns Hopkins University Press, 1979.

Dave Grossman. *On Killing: The Psychological Cost of Learning to Kill in War and Society.* Back Bay Books, 1996.

Barbara Hall. "Madam Secretary." CBS, 2014-present.

Pete Hamil. "The Death and Life of John Lennon." *New York Magazine,* Dec. 20, 1980.

John Hayward. "Hillary Clinton: Muslims Are 'Peaceful and Tolerant,' Have Nothing Whatsoever to Do with Terrorism." *Breitbart London,* Nov. 19, 2015.

"Sarah Kissling Hendrix Obituary." Lexington *Herald Leader,* Feb. 21, 2015.

Tsangnyon Heurica, Andrew Quintman, and Donald S. Lopez, Jr. *The Life of Milarepa.* Penguin, 2010.

Homer. *The Iliad.* Richard Lattimore, tr. University of Chicago Press, 2011.

_____. *The Odyssey.* Richard Lattimore, tr. Harper Perennial Modern Classics, 2007.

Richard Hugo. *Making Certain It Goes On: The Collected Poems.* Norton, 1991.

Roland Joffe. "The Killing Fields." Screenplay, Bruce Robinson. Enigma Productions, 1984.

Kurt Johnson and Robert David Ord. *The Coming Interspiritual Age.* Namaste, 2013.

Mark Johnson. "A Word with You." Milwaukee-Wisconsin *Journal Sentinel,* Dec. 3, 2015.

Sonya Jones. "Our sheriff, our hero, our protector: Sam Catron's mother, brother say why he was so respected." Somerset *Commonwealth Journal,* May 3, 2002.

_____, guest ed. "Psychoanalysis and Cinema. *Film Criticism*, Spring 1990.

_____. *Small Claims, Large Encounters.* Brito & Lair, 1995.

Krzysztof Kieslowski. "The Decalogue." Sender Freis Berlin, Telewizja Polska, Zespot Filmowy, 1988.

"Killing John Lennon." CNN Special Report, Dec. 4, 2015.

John Killinger. *Hemingway and the Dead Gods.* University of Kentucky Press, 1960.

Martin Luther King, Jr. *Letters to a Birmingham Jail: A Response to the Words and Dreams of Martin Luther King, Jr.* Bryan Loritts, ed. Moody Publishers, 2014.

Robert King and Michelle King. "The Good Wife." CBS, 2009-present.

Stanley Kubrick. Forward to Kieslowski and Piesiewicz. *Decalogue: The Ten Commandments.* Faber & Faber, 1991.

Spike Lee. "Chi-Raq." 40 Acres & A Mule Filmworks, Amazon Studios, 2015.

John Lennon and Yoko Ono. "Imagine." YouTube.

Denise Levertov. *Selected Poems*. New Directions, 2002.

Muhsin Mahdi, ed. *The Arabian Nights*. Husain Haddawy, tr. Norton, 2008.

Louis Malle. "My Dinner with Andre." Screenplay, Wallace Shawn and Andrew Gregory. George W. George and Beverly Karp, 1981.

Dean Manning. "Answers trickle in about murder involving Union professor." *The Mountain Advocate*, Dec. 26, 2015.

Thomas Merton. *Conjectures of a Guilty Bystander*. Image Books, 1968.

Matthew Mitchell. "UK Wildcat Women's Basketball." ESPN 3, SEC Network, 2007-present.

Nancy Mullane. *Life After Murder: Five Men in Search of Redemption*. Public Affairs, 2012.

Ryan Murphy. "Eat, Pray, Love." Columbia Pictures, 2010.

Bridgette Leben Nacos. *Mass-Mediated Terrorism: The Central Role of the Media in Terrorism and Counterterrorism*. Roman & Littlefield, 2007.

R.K. Narayan. *The Ramayana*. Vision Books, 2006.

Laszlo Nemes. "Son of Saul." Sony Pictures, 2015.

Jonathan Nolan. "Person of Interest." CBS, 2011-present.

Paul Overberg et al. "Behind the Bloodshed." *USA Today,* Dec. 4, 2013.

Alan J. Paluka. "All the President's Men." Warner Brothers, 1976.

Danielle Paquette. "Why Young American Women Are Joining ISIS." *The Washington Post,* Nov. 17, 2015.

Sean Penn. "El Chapo Speaks: A secret visit with the most wanted man in the world." *Rolling Stone,* Jan. 9, 2016.

"Public Service Announcements." National Basketball Association and Everytown for Gun Safety, Dec. 25, 2015.

Phillip Resnick. "Child Murder by Parents: A Psychiatric Review of Filicide." *American Journal of Psychiatry,* 126: 1969.

Adrienne Rich. *The Dream of a Common Language.* Norton, 1977.

Rainer Maria Rilke. *Letters to a Young Poet.* Merchant Books, 2012.

Chogyam Trungpa Rinpoche. *Smile at Fear.* Carolyn Rose Gimian, ed. Shambhala, 2009.

Charlie Rose and Sean Penn. "60 Minutes." CBS, Jan. 17, 2016.

"San Bernardino Massacre." CNN Newscasts, Dec. 2-16, 2015.

Jean-Paul Sartre. *No Exit*. Samuel French, Inc., 1958.

Piero Scaruffi. "The worst genocides of the 20th and 21st centuries." scaruffi.com

Sydney Schanberg. *The Death and Life of Dith Pran*. Penguin, 1980.

Brian Schatz. "Inside Anonymous' Messy Cyberwar Against ISIS." *Mother Jones,* Nov. 24, 2015.

Arthur Schopenhauer. *The World as Will and Idea*. David Berman, ed. Everyman Paperbacks, 1995.

William Shakespeare. *The Oxford Shakespeare*. Stanley Wells, ed. Oxford University Press, 2005.

Sw. Shantananda with Peggy Bendet. *The Splendor of Recognition*. SYDA, 2003.

Sw. Shraddhananda aka Dr. Sonya Jones. *Jesus Was a Shaktipat Guru*. The Sacred Feet Publishing Imprint, 2014.

Scott Simon. "After Murder: Learning to Live After You've Killed." *NPR Books,* 2012.

Kristina Smith. "Funeral arrangements set for Hendrix family." *Times Tribune,* Feb. 18, 2015.

Gloria Steinem. *Outrageous Acts and Everyday Rebellions*. Holt Paperbacks, 1995.

Jessica Stern. *Terror in the Name of God: Why Religious Militants Kill.* Harper Perennial, 2004.

Jessica Stern and J.M. Berger. *ISIS: The State of Terror.* Ecco, 2015.

Oliver Stone. "Natural Born Killers." Warner Brothers, 1994.

Maria Szalavitz. "Psychiatrist Phillip Resnick on Why Parents Kill Their Own Kids." *Time,* Feb. 1, 2011.

Rajendra Tandon. *Valmiki's Ramayana.* Rupa Publications India, 2013.

Sabrina Tavernise. "In Missouri, Fewer Gun Restrictions and More Killings." *The New York Times,* Dec. 22, 2015.

Wayne Teasdale. *The Mystic Heart.* New World Library, 1999.

"The Famous Salem Coven Witch Photo." *National Geographic,* April 1979.

Dalton Trumbo. *Johnny Got His Gun.* J.P. Lippincott, 1939.

_____. "Johnny Got His Gun." Screenplay , Dalton Trumbo and Luis Brunel. Bruce Campbell, 1971.

Vyasa. *The Bhagavad Gita.* Barbara Stoller Miller. Bantam Classics. 1986.

_____. *The Mahabharata.* Penguin Classics. 2009.

John Walsh. "The Hunt." CNN, 2014-present.

Michael Weiss and Hassan Hassan. *ISIS: Inside the Army of Terror.* Regan Arts, 2015.

Elizabeth Weitzman. Photographs of Woody Harrelson, Sheila Metzler. "Mother Nature's Son." *Breathe,* March/April 2005.

Eudora Welty. *The Optimist's Daughter.* Random House, 1986.

William Carlos Williams. *Selected Essays.* New Directions, 1969.

Marianne Williamson. "America, ISIL, and the Power of Atonement," "On ISIL." marianne.com

David Sloan Wilson. *Does Altruism Exist?* Yale University/Templeton Press, 2015.

Dick Wolf. "Law and Order." USA Television, NBC Universal Television, Universal Television, 1990-present.

Graeme Wood. "What ISIS Really Wants." *The Atlantic,* 2015.

About the Author

Photo by Melissa Reid

Rev. Dr. Sw. Shraddhananda (aka Sonya Jones), a member of the Saraswati Order of Monastics and Meditation Masters, serves as Spiritual Director of Slate Branch Ashram in Kentucky. She also teaches in the Honors Program at the University of Kentucky and serves as Preceptor and Lineage Holder for The Community of The Mystic Heart. She holds a Ph.D. from Emory University and is a Distinguished Alumni Scholar at Union College, her undergraduate alma mater. The author of numerous books and papers, she has lectured on six continents.

www.ingramcontent.com/pod-product-compliance
Lightning Source LLC
Chambersburg PA
CBHW021405090426
42742CB00009B/1016